Pickwick's Progress

Pickwick's Progress

A Centenary History of the City Pickwick Club
(1909–2009)

Ina Taylor

Ellingham Press

ISBN 978-0-9547560-6-2

Published by Ellingham Press

www.ellinghampress.co.uk

Ellingham Press, 43 High Street, Much Wenlock, Shropshire
TF13 6AD

Typeset by ISB Typesetting, Sheffield, UK

www.sheffieldtypesetting.com

Printed on acid-free paper by CPI Antony Rowe, Chippenham

Contents

This history
Is
Dedicated to
CHARLES JOHN HUFFAM DICKENS Esq
(1806–1870)
Without whose GENIUS there would have
been no SAMUEL PICKWICK Esq G.C.M.P.C.
To
SIR JAMES ROLL
(1847–1927)
Without whose IMAGINATION & ENTERPRISE
there would be no CITY PICKWICK CLUB
And to
SIR PETER GADSDEN
(1929–2006)
Without whose ENERGY & INSPIRATION
PICKWICK'S PROGRESS
May never have seen the
Light of Day

Foreword

As the current President it is my great privilege and pleasure to introduce 'Pickwick's Progress', a Centenary History of the City Pickwick Club, 1909–2009.

This excellent book was the inspiration of my illustrious predecessor, the late Sir Peter Gadsden. In 2006 he formed the Book Committee consisting of five literary Pickwickians, with Maurice Cocking ('Whiffin') as chairman. They commissioned Sir Peter's biographer, the distinguished author Ina Taylor, to write the Club's history. Membership of that august group seems to have been somewhat unlucky, even hazardous, in that Sir Peter Gadsden, John Williams and Tom Wilmot all passed to Dingley Dell! As a result, Maurice Cocking, together with the other survivor, Christopher Giles, were joined by Andrew Whitton (the new 'Snodgrass') and myself (the new 'Mr Pickwick').

I take this opportunity to thank the many members who have assisted the Committee and our author by providing much of the information that now appears in print. In this regard, particular mention must again be made of Maurice Cocking who, having joined in 1967, is the longest serving member of the Club and fortunately has an excellent memory.

Readers will discover that, unlike the frailty of its individual members, the City Pickwick Club has not only survived during the past century but thrived. The excellent attendance at our meetings, the quality of our speakers, the distinguished guests and the existence of a substantial waiting list for membership of the Club, all suggest that enjoyment of the works of Charles Dickens in general and the Pickwick Papers in particular continues unabated and indicate that the Club has a bright future.

Samuel Pickwick
(John Chalstrey)

Acknowledgements

I have been very grateful to so many people for helping me uncover the hundred years of the City Pickwick Club's existence, but one name stands out above all others: Maurice Cocking (Whiffin). He has been my constant adviser from the outset, giving me the benefit of the longest personal membership of the City Pickwick Club, offering helpful ideas and suggesting possible avenues of approach when blank walls loomed, but best of all he kept me hugely entertained with his wonderful wit. Thank you, Whiffin.

Thanks also have to go to the other members of the original book committee now enjoying companionship in Dingley Dell: the late Sir Peter Gadsden (the 8th Mr Pickwick), who suggested this book and provided me with information and contacts; the late John Williams (Serjeant Buzfuz), who was an enthusiastic supporter of the research, ferreting out useful snippets from Guildhall archives to aid the project and the late Tom Wilmott (Mr Potts), an extremely supportive member of that original committee.

I owe a debt of gratitude to those who stepped in to continue their good work and steer the project through to completion. I am most grateful to the Club's Hon Sec Andrew Whitton (Augustus Snodgrass) for much of the book's behind the scenes co-ordination and for swiftly providing email responses to my many queries and to Sir John Chalstrey (the 9th Mr Pickwick) for his continuing support. I must thank Christopher Giles (Sam Weller), who, as an earlier Augustus Snodgrass, gave me access to his excellent records along with earlier records from the Club's archives. His kind invitation to lunch with him at the George and Vulture gave me a personal insight into the flavour of that delightful hostelry. The late Cedric Dickens (Joseph Smiggers) also showed me hospitality whilst giving me the benefit of his knowledge and networking skills with other Pickwick Clubs around the globe. I am also grateful for David Wootton's (Mr Wicks) help in sorting out the contractual aspects of the project.

Thanks are due to the National Portrait Gallery for providing a photograph of Sir Frederick Rowland; to the Worshipful Company of Butchers for supplying a copy of their painting of W Fred Bonser; to Alastair Collett for supplying a photograph of Sir Kingsley Collett; to Neville Wells for information and photographs of his father Major Stanley Wells; to the Dickens House Museum for kind permission to reproduce the photograph of Moses Pickwick's clock; to the archivist at the Worshipful Company of Barbers; to Hector Goldsack for scanning and restoring some difficult early photographs and to Michael de Silva for supplying those fascinating extracts from the first Minute Book of the City Pickwick Club which appear in Appendix 1.

I have thoroughly enjoyed the detective work involved in this book and am grateful to everyone for their good humour and willingness to assist. It has been a privilege for me to be able to enjoy a little of the genial company for which the City Pickwick Club is famed.

A Hundred Years of the City Pickwick Club

The Posthumous Papers of the Pickwick Club were greeted with muted enthusiasm when they first appeared as monthly instalments in April 1836. It was the appearance of Samuel Weller in the fifth number that transformed things. *Pickwick Papers* became hugely popular and the fortunes of Charles Dickens soared overnight. Public imagination was captivated by the jovial activities of this band of friends; not only were their exploits followed and discussed in every coffee shop and tavern, but a few groups were set up with similar ideas in mind. An article about London Literary Dining Clubs said, 'London is so full of literary clubs that one cannot deal with them all.' The reason for this, it said, was that 'winter nights … are particularly alluring in literary centres, where, generally, food is a secondary consideration, and the after-dinner speaking the first'.

By 1900 Dickens had his fair share of clubs. A speaker at the City Pickwick Club in 1989 told members that the first City Pickwick Club was founded in 1837 and used to meet at the Sun Tavern in Longacre, but nothing further is known of this early club. There was a Boz Club 'formed from fragments of Dickens' surviving friends who knew him in the flesh'. They dined at the Athenaeum Club and included luminaries such as artists Marcus Stone and Luke Fildes along with Dickens' son Henry Fielding Dickens.

The Pickwick Bicycle Club established in 1870 (more details of the earliest surviving Pickwick Club appear later) was mentioned with W T Charley QC as its president. Another club referred to was the Pickwick Social Society founded in 1897. They held monthly meetings 'for social evenings, reading the master's work, interspersed with music and conversation' and had a charitable purpose, 'to assist deserving cases'. The Cheerybles Club, for the Dickens fraternity, held regular concerts.

Dickens had also spawned overseas clubs by 1900. One in Boston had been founded by a woman. Mrs Adelaide Garland

established the Dickens Ladies Club in 1894 which boasted 80 members. The Columbian Pickwick Club, also in the USA, had its headquarters in a building designed to replicate the Great White Horse Inn at Ipswich.

According to a newspaper of the day dining clubs had begun to slump by 1908 because 'the man stays at home by choice', but the City Pickwick Club begged to differ. Fascination with this companionable, early nineteenth-century world of coaching where groups of friends travelled round the country inspired some light-hearted imitators. This was particularly true of those who had a penchant for driving a coach and horses or enjoyed meeting up for convivial dining.

It was pleasure in the works of Dickens combined with his favourite pastime, driving a coach-and-four, that inspired James Roll to form the Pickwick Coaching Club at the beginning of the twentieth century. Alderman Roll possessed his own coach *Vigilant* which he used to commute between Boxhill and Victoria. He also thought nothing of driving to Brighton and was a familiar sight with his 'four-in-hand' around the home counties. His Pickwick Coaching Club was limited to twelve members, being the number who could comfortably fit on *Vigilant*. These were largely drawn from fellow-employees of the Pearl Life Assurance Company, where he was chairman. Alderman Roll took the soubriquet Mr Pickwick. Additionally there were Mr Foley (Nathaniel Winkle), Mr C Webster (Tracy Tupman), Mr T H Wye CC (Lieutenant Tappleton), Mr H P Monckton CC (Bob Sawyer), Sir Edward Cooper (Mr Wardle) and

James Roll, the first Mr Pickwick, is seen here with his personal coach Vigilant *which he drove daily from his home in Boxhill to business in Victoria in the early years of the twentieth century.*

Mr F D Bowles JP CC (Mr Dodson). Details of the other five members have not survived.

The Pickwick Coaching Club only met once a year, but their meeting lasted for several days. Members climbed aboard the *Vigilant*. Alderman Roll took up his whip and, like their namesakes, the intrepid explorers set off allegedly to visit every place associated with Dickens 'one by one'. Roll entered fully into the spirit of Pickwick and laid down rules that were to be kept. One was that 'on all State occasions', by which he meant breakfast, lunch and dinner, each member had to be addressed by their proper sou-briquet. Any infringement was subject to a fine of sixpence 'to be paid forthwith to Mr Grundy, and to be disposed of by him as he alone shall think fit; his decision to be final'.

The exploits of the coaching club came to an end in 1913 when Roll was in his sixty-sixth year. The advent of the First World War prevented the scheduled 1914 outing and coaching excursions were never resumed. The outings had clearly been huge fun because one member gave Mr Pickwick a three-handled silver loving cup inscribed *Presented to J Roll, Esq., C.C. (Samuel Pickwick, Esq) by an old member of the Club as a token of his high esteem and regard for the many and happy coaching days we have spent in the company of our friends.* Although James Roll's coaching days were over, his delight in Dickens continued unabated. He had already become a member of Charles Dickens Lodge (no. 2757) in Loughton, Essex, in 1902, going on to serve as master. He had close associations with the Dickens Fellowship, founded in 1902, but Roll is not recorded as a member.

The First Mr Pickwick

Sir *James Roll Bt*, *the founder of the City Pickwick Club and the first Mr Pickwick. He was described as 'a man of simple tastes, devoid of side, endowed with a keen sense of humour … who insisted on a glossy well-ironed topper, liked a glass of whisky and had a fondness for driving a well-turned-out team of horses'. From humble beginnings in East Anglia, he rose to become chairman of the Pearl Assurance Company and Lord Mayor in 1920. He was created a baronet in 1921.*

Sir James Roll Bt – Mr Pickwick 1909–27

What is of particular interest to us was Roll's decision early in 1909 to form a dining club called the City Pickwick Club. 'The object of the club is to perpetuate the memory of Charles Dickens,' he announced. Members of the Pickwick Coaching Club were amongst the early members and others joined them. A full list of the founding members can be found at Appendix 1. Other early members included Mr Bransby Williams 'the Showman' (a character actor who specialised in performing monologues of Dickensian characters around the music halls), Mr C H Green (who is listed as the honorary secretary of the Dickens Fellowship showing the close relationship between these two organisations in the early days), John Gardner, licensee of the *George and Vulture*, and Louis 'Chance' Newton, a journalist on *The Referee*. Initially membership was set at 30, but that had to be increased to 50 by March 1911 and 60 in October 1913.

It is noticeable that from the outset membership included distinguished members of the Corporation of the City of London. The club could soon boast three aldermen amongst its members and in the autumn of 1909, the year of its foundation, Alderman Roll became sheriff and Lord Mayor in 1920. Other early members of the City Pickwick Club also held high office: Sir Edward Cooper (Mr Wardle) became Lord Mayor in 1919 and Colonel Sir Louis Newton in 1923.

The City Pickwick Club's inaugural dinner was held on 16th March 1909, naturally at the *George and Vulture*, which would continue to be their abode for the next hundred years. When Mr Pickwick (James Roll) became Lord Mayor the club was invited to dine at the Mansion House.

The City Pickwick Club's meetings continued during the First World War, but one member was killed by enemy action in 1916. Early in the 1920s meetings were in full swing and described as 'thoroughly Dickensian in character'. In addition to the dinner, there was a silent tribute to the memory of Charles Dickens and some form of entertainment.

In October 1920 it was recorded that Mr Bransby Williams needed little persuasion from fellow club members to 'declaim with wonderful fidelity' the famous speech of Sergeant Buzfuz to the jury in the Bardell case. The 49-year-old actor had already made a

A sketch of the famous speech of Sergeant Buzfuz in the case of Bardell versus Pickwick made during the London Theatre's production of Pickwick Papers.

name for himself at the Empire music hall in Leicester Square with his presentation of Scrooge, Uriah Heep and Little Nell's grandfather. However it was his impersonation of Tony Weller, the stagecoach driver in *Pickwick Papers*, which went down particularly well with the City Pickwick Club. Williams is reported to have appeared in Dickensian costume, coughing and spluttering as he advised his son Sam against marriage and to 'beware of widows'. As late as March 1957 the club noted 'that grand old veteran Bransby Williams', then aged 86, had entertained members and guests with his famous Sergeant Buzfuz speech.

The fact that Mr Williams was still a member decades later shows how much people valued their membership of the City

Bransby William Pharez *(1870–1961), known in the music hall as Bransby Williams, was famed for his portrayal of Dickensian characters and was also one of the earliest members of the City Pickwick Club.*

Pickwick Club. Such longevity of membership is not exceptional and early records often show fathers and sons maintaining a long unbroken association with the club as they do today.

Dinners at the *George and Vulture* regularly featured a 'Pickwickian programme of music' slotted between the speeches. A surviving menu from November 1938 shows members were entertained by Miss Esther Coleman (contralto) and Mr Colin Cunningham (tenor) accompanied on the piano by Mr Frederick Arthur. Mr Will Kings is also listed on the programme as 'entertainer', but it is not clear how he entertained. These musical features died out in the 1950s.

From its earliest days, the City Pickwick Club was concerned to preserve things associated with Charles Dickens. The chair-

This painting of the George and Vulture *by Paul Braddon was given to the City Pickwick Club by Bransby Williams.*

man always gave a toast to 'The Immortal Memory of Charles Dickens' and the guest speaker responded. At a meeting in 1920 one member drew the club's attention to the sale of the Leather Bottle at Cobham and the Bull Hotel at Rochester, suggesting that 'each should be acquired by some coteries of lovers of Dickens in order that the characteristics of the two houses might be

Founder of the City Pickwick Club, James Roll, presented this clock to the Dickens House Museum. The clock once belonged to coach proprietor Moses Pickwick, who had offices at the White Hart Inn, Bath. Dickens would have known Mr Pickwick from coach journeys to Bath and, years later, he borrowed his name for the famous Posthumous Papers.

preserved without any diminution'. Sadly there is no reference to the outcome of this splendid idea.

The City Pickwick Club maintained a close link with the Dickens Fellowship and members often belonged to both organisations. There were also good links with Dickens societies abroad such that in 1921 the president of the Dickens Fellowship in Melbourne, Australia, was pleased to attend the *George and Vulture* and address the club.

The Second Mr Pickwick

No picture survives of John Herbert Bishop, the second Mr Pick-
wick. This sketch of Mr Pickwick illustrated Bell's Life in London
in 1838 and has remained the archetypal idea of what Mr Samuel
Pickwick should look like.

John Herbert Bishop – Mr Pickwick 1927–36

Following Sir James Roll's death in 1927, Herbert Bishop, as he liked to be called, took over as the second Mr Pickwick. He had been a member of the Worshipful Company of Barbers since 1921, but records for this period of the City Pickwick Club have not survived and no picture of Mr Bishop has come to light. He is said to have been a 'powerful influence in the City and in several livery companies' but failed to achieve high office because of poor health.

It was during Mr Bishop's presidency that the City Pickwick Club was faced with eviction from the *George and Vulture*. During the 1930s stories circulated that the ancient building was to be closed and demolished – a threat that Pickwickians sadly grew all too familiar with throughout the twentieth century. At that time the freehold was owned by Williams Deacon's Bank and it was rumoured they had sold it to a 'commercial interest' which planned to pull the hostelry down. When the story was taken up by the City Press, the bank issued a statement saying 'they had not even thought of destroying a property that, apart from its historic value, is doing a splendid trade'. So the *George and Vulture* survived to fight another closure battle and the City Pickwick Club breathed a sigh of relief.

In March 1936 the Club decided to celebrate the centenary of the publication of *Pickwick Papers* and Herbert Bishop took the chair at the Pickwick Centenary Dinner which was held at Girdlers' Hall. Apart from the Mansion House dinner, this was the first time the club had moved away from the *George and Vulture* for one of its dinners but the splendour of a livery company's hall seemed appropriate for the occasion. This became a pattern for special events in the future when more space for guests and more luxurious catering were needed.

Only a few months after the centenary dinner Herbert Bishop died and the mantle of Mr Pickwick passed to another. Family contact with the Bishop family continued until the outbreak of the Second World War through the membership of two of Herbert's sons.

The Third Mr Pickwick

W Fred Bonser OBE, *the third Mr Pickwick, was a popular and genial personality. He is seen here as Master of the Worshipful Company of Butchers and he was also a member of the Horners' Company and Barbers' Livery Company.*

W Fred Bonser – Mr Pickwick 1936–54

Fred Bonser took over in 1936 and continued the pattern of meetings already established. Subscriptions remained at one guinea per year with new members required to pay a guinea entrance fee. A menu from November 1938 shows that musical entertainment continued to be a significant part of a normal evening meeting and the account book for that year notes the pianist received £1 6s 3d for entertaining the diners.

The club was thriving. Membership stood at 57 in 1938 with a further ten people on the waiting list for the following year. The prospect of war was looming and in the event only four had time to join in 1939 before the club was forced to close. They held their last dinner at the *George and Vulture* on 13th March 1939 and, like everything else in the City, closed down for the duration of the war.

On 14th November 1949 the City Pickwick Club was back. Their first dinner at the *George and Vulture* was featured in a December edition of *The Tatler*.

Menu.	Artistes.
Royal Native Oysters.	Miss ESTER COLEMAN, Contralto.
Thick Ox Tail Soup.	Mr. COLIN CUNNINGHAM, Tenor.
Fried Dover Sole.	
Roast Saddle of Mutton, Potatoes in Jackets. Brussels Sprouts.	Mr. WILL KINGS, Entertainer.
Apple Tart.	Accompanist, Mr. FREDERICK ARTHUR.
Stilton Cheese.	
Coffee.	Chairman: Sir JOHN PAKEMAN, C.B.E., C.C. (Mr. Dobson.)
November 14th, 1938.	

Menu 1938 Dinner

Fred Bonser, flanked on his left by Sir Cuthbert Whitaker (editor of Whitaker's Almanac) *and on his right by Capt C B Sanders RNVR. On the table in front of Mr Pickwick stands the Club's prized possession, a Georgian punch bowl which graced the table at special dinners. The club's first meeting since its disbandment for war was undoubtedly such an event.*

The Fourth Mr Pickwick

Sir Frederick Rowland Bt was a City accountant before his retirement. He had also taken a very active part in civic life serving as Chief Commoner in 1936, Sheriff in 1938 and Lord Mayor in 1949. He had been Master of the Worshipful Company of Horners between 1935 and 1937.

Sir Frederick Rowland Bt – Mr Pickwick 1954–59

In 1954 Fred Bonser decided it was time to retire as Mr Pickwick. He was replaced by 80-year-old Sir Frederick Rowland, who as 'Mr Roker' had been a member of the City Pickwick Club since October 1938. Rowland was a Somerset man by birth and an accountant by profession, who had lived and worked in the square mile since 1900. Like many Pickwick Club members he took a very active part in City life, serving as member of Common Council for the Ward of Cordwainer since 1922 and as Chief Commoner in 1936. He was elected Sheriff in 1938, shortly after he had joined the City Pickwick Club, and became Lord Mayor in 1949. He had been Master of the Worshipful Company of Horners in 1935–6 and 1936–7.

By Sir Frederick's time the menu for Pickwick dinners had settled into a pattern that has remained for around 40 years. (At a dinner in 1994 the curator of the Dickens House Museum explained to members that the basis of their traditional menu had

TOASTS

THE QUEEN

"THE IMMORTAL MEMORY
OF CHARLES DICKENS"

*"It would be better to dewote the liquor to vishin you success
and prosperity"*

Proposed by: ALDERMAN KENNETH CORK, F.C.A.

THE GUESTS

"They've the advantage of me in numbers"

Proposed by: THOS. GROFFIN
                              (John H. B. Clover)

Response by: A. E. GASKELL, B.A., A.L.A

THE CLUB AND THE CHAIRMAN

"You're worse than any of 'em"

Proposed by: SIR THOS. CLUBBER
                              (John G. Gapp, D.L., C.C.)

Response by: THE CHAIRMAN

MENU

"I never see men eat and drink so much afore"

Smoked Salmon

Thick Ox Tail Soup

Pickwick Pudding
Baked Potatoes in Jackets
Brussels Sprouts

Apple and Cranberry Tart

Stilton Cheese and Biscuits

Coffee

"They're only looking for their hats"

Menu 1958 Dinner

come from a cookery book written anonymously by Charles Dickens' wife.) Royal native oysters opened the proceedings and were followed by thick oxtail soup. The additional fish course of pre-war days disappeared from the menu and guests moved on to a new delicacy called Pickwick pudding which was a hearty meal of steak and kidney with a suet crust. The suet crust continued until 1994 when the steamer at the *George and Vulture* broke down. Because Fortes the caterers had been served notice to quit, the steamer was never replaced. Instead a pastry crust was substituted and Pickwick pudding became Pickwick pie.

In pre-war days the menu had featured English roasts like saddle of mutton. Jacket potatoes remained on the menu, but the apple tart became more adventurous with the addition of cranberries. Some excellent Stilton followed and fine wines naturally remained an important part of the dinner. Members paid 30 shillings for their dinner which was supplied by the caterer John Gardner & Co.

It was still customary for members to arrive dressed in morning suits at 6.15 pm to enjoy 'wanities' followed by dinner at 6.30 *precisely*. Music remained a part of dinners but was largely confined to some piano accompaniment for the final rousing rendition of Auld Lang Syne at 8.45 to close the meeting.

Like many members of the City Pickwick Club, it was a case of son following in father's footsteps. Wentworth Rowland became a member in 1951 and when his father became Mr Pickwick, Wentworth Rowland took his father's soubriquet of Tom Roker and served the club well for many years. He became chairman during his father's presidency and subsequently, as Augustus Snodgrass, served as secretary.

Sadly Sir Frederick Rowland's tenure as Mr Pickwick was one of the shortest as he died in November 1959. His legacy was the president's badge which he presented to the club. This silver-gilt and enamel badge has been proudly displayed on Mr Pickwick's chest ever since, but Sir Frederick's generosity was not officially recognised until 1972 when an inscription was added by his successor, Major Stanley Wells. The badge is displayed in full Pickwickian glory on the front cover of this History.

*The President's badge was the gift of the 4th Mr
Pickwick, Sir Frederick Rowland Bt.*

The Fifth Mr Pickwick

Major Stanley Wells MBE *photographed here in 1949 when he was elected Sheriff and the same year he joined the City Pickwick Club. He played a very active role in City life representing Cripplegate Ward, as Chief Commoner, founder of the Launderers' Livery Company, Master of the Tallow Chandlers and a host of other City offices.*

Major Stanley Walter Wells – Mr Pickwick 1959–73

Major Wells belonged to a new breed of Pickwickians. He had joined the City Pickwick Club in October 1949 as Mr Wardle once meetings resumed after the Second World War. He had already served the City well by this time as member for the Ward of Cripplegate and Chief Commoner, to mention but two offices. At the time of his election to the club he was about to hold office as Sheriff.

During his time of office the club saw several changes which brought it firmly into post-war Britain. One of those was the change from morning suits to business suits which was more convenient for members coming straight from their offices to dine at the *George and Vulture.*

Out went the entertainment that lingered from earlier times. Ming Chow the 'Light-Fingered One' seems to have been one of the last of the entertainers at an evening dinner in 1961 – one wonders whether his name had anything to do with that decision! More likely it was getting difficult to finish at a sensible time to enable members to catch the train home. Speeches and toasts were an established part of the evening with some entertaining and prestigious speakers. As the tone of the club was changing, a speaker was more in keeping with the times than a well-meaning pianist and contralto.

This was also a time when outings to theatres were arranged for members. Sixty members and friends went to a production at the Mermaid Theatre in June 1960 and dined together, but unfortunately did not record what they saw.

During Major Wells's time members of the Dickens family also played a greater role in the life of the City Pickwick Club. Naturally they were active supporters of the Dickens Fellowship, but had been less involved with the dining club. Perhaps the accent on good speakers and less on Chinese conjurors lured them in.

Sir Henry Fielding Dickens, Common Serjeant of the City of London, was a regular visitor to the club in the mid 1950s and his brother Philip Charles Dickens, Cedric's father, became a member for a short time. Although Cedric Dickens was not a member at this time, he was in touch with the City Pickwick Club in the 1960s. He organised a Pickwick picnic in the summer of 1965 which a few club members attended so the following year he invited the club to 'a bigger and better one'.

Several scenes in Dickens' Pickwick Papers *were set inside the* George and Vulture *like this one.*

It was also during Major Wells's time as Mr Pickwick that it became the custom for the Lord Mayor to visit the club. Whilst it was not unknown for members of the City Pickwick Club to become Lord Mayors, until 1963 it seems no Lord Mayor had made a particular point of including a visit to the club on their official itinerary. In 1963 when Bob Sawyer (Sir Ralph Perring) rose to that office it is recorded that he suggested the Lord Mayor, attended by his Sheriffs, should 'assist at our dinner'. A letter of the following year from Augustus Snodgrass (Sir Wentworth Rowland) also mentions this event. 'Only once before in the Annals of the Club which takes its name from that of its Inspired Leader, have the Lord Mayor and Sheriffs assisted at a "snug little Dinner" with the Members. This was during March 1963 when Bob Sawyer so graced our Board.' Snoddy goes on to say, 'On March 9th 1964,

Benjamin Allen (the Rt Hon. The Lord Mayor) attended by his Sheriffs, will honour us with his presence.' On that occasion the Lord Mayor who sat down to dine with his fellow Pickwickians was Alderman C J Harman.

Pressure on the Lord Mayor's time has meant that these occasions were rare. The Lord Mayor in 1966 was club member Mr Namby (Sir Robert Bellinger) and he too dined with his officers and members at the *George and Vulture*, but a note from Augustus Snodgrass records what would become the pattern for the future. 'The Rt Hon. The Lord Mayor and the Queen's Sheriffs called in upon the Members assembled and tarried awhile taking a wanity before proceeding about their lawful occasion elsewhere.' It was indeed a pity that the Lord Mayor and his retinue were unable to dine with the club, but the fact that a visit to the City Pickwick Club had become a fixture in the Mayoral diary says a great deal about the club's standing in the City. It was not long before it became customary on these Mayoral visits for the club to present the Lord Mayor with a cheque for his chosen charity.

The period of the fifth Mr Pickwick's office coincided with celebrations to commemorate Charles Dickens' 150th birthday, an event the City Pickwick Club would celebrate in style. Eighty-eight members and their guests sat down to a splendid dinner at the Tallow Chandlers' Hall on 6th November 1962. For this occasion music graced the evening with a recital by students from the Guildhall School of Music and Drama. Henry Charles Dickens represented the Dickens family since none of them were in membership at that time, and the Immortal Memory was proposed by V C Clinton-Baddeley.

Another significant event occurred at this time: 'Pickwick' the musical was staged at the Saville Theatre in 1965 with Harry Secombe in the starring role. The City Pickwick Club made contact with the famous actor to invite him to dine with them and he in turn issued an invitation for Mr Pickwick and Augustus Snodgrass to attend a stage party when the show closed in London before its transfer to America. In the event Mr Pickwick was not able to attend and his place was taken by Sergeant Buzfuz. Harry Secombe was delighted by their attendance and took the opportunity to present the club with a plaque and to loan the club a prayer book that had once belonged to Joseph Pickwick, the stagecoach proprietor.

As a mark of their thanks for such generosity, the Pickwick committee voted unanimously to grant Harry Secombe honorary membership of the club when he was next able to visit. That visit did not happen for another two years because Mr Secombe was on the other side of the Atlantic and then involved in a television show, but in March 1967 he did honour the club by dining at the *George and Vulture.* His proposal of 'The Immortal Memory of Charles Dickens' was much enjoyed. Clearly Mr Secombe valued their invitation and was generous to the City Pickwick Club, presenting them with a letter from Phiz and two volumes of an illustrated *Pickwick Papers*, promising to follow that up with the presentation of a first edition of the great work. The first edition did follow and members asked Harry Secombe to inscribe the flyleaf. In the background the committee worried about whether the club's insurance policy was adequate for such a valuable book!

Despite the exciting events that took place during Major Stanley Wells's period of office, membership and attendance were issues that occupied the committee. Membership during the 1960s hovered around 60, but dinners at the *George and Vulture* struggled to muster 30 and on occasions only 20 sat down to dine. What irritated the committee most was not just that some members never showed up but that many did not have the courtesy to reply to invitations to dine at the club.

It was during a discussion about membership that in true Pickwickian fashion, Major Wells stood on his chair and told the club 'it was all very well for members to pay their guests the compliment of asking them if they would like to join, but with a waiting list of ten, and only one or two vacancies in membership pending, we must be careful only to select as members those persons who were genuinely interested in the club and what it stood for as well as able, and of a mind, to attend regularly at meetings.'

These were years when rapid inflation became endemic, which meant the club regularly found itself having to notch up the cost of dinner and subscriptions. In 1965 subscriptions rose to 3 guineas and continued on up to 5 guineas four years later. Dinner prices also rose to 37/6 in November 1966, 45/- the year after, to £2.50 in 1971, £3 the following year and £4 the year after.

During 1972 Major Stanley Wells did not enjoy good health and felt it was time to hand over the duties of Mr Pickwick to another. He informed the committee that autumn that he had invited Sir Kingsley Collett CBE to take his place subject to the approval of

This illustration of Mr Pickwick standing on his chair to address his col-leagues has been regularly re-enacted at meetings of the club over the years. The minutes record the fifth Mr Pickwick 'now standing on his chair in his accustomed manner … Despite having his coat-tails pulled, Mr Pickwick went on, and voiced the opinion held by many that the Club should be more selective in its choice of members.'

members. 'Tom' Collett, as he liked to be known, was a popular choice and members were unanimous in their support. At the first meeting of the new year, Major Wells handed his badge of office over to 'Mr Wardle' who now took the famous soubriquet Mr Pickwick. The club presented their outgoing president with a silver Pickwick plate engraved with the illustration 'Christmas Eve at Mr Wardle's' and inscribed *Major Stanley W Wells MBE 'Mr Pickwick' 1959-1973. From members of the City Pickwick Club with affection.*

The Sixth Mr Pickwick

Sir Thomas Kingsley Collett, *whose father had been Lord Mayor of London in 1933–4, represented the Ward of Bridge and served on many City committees. He was member of the Worshipful Company of Distillers and had been Master in 1960–1.*

Sir Thomas Kingsley Collett, CBE – Mr Pickwick 1973–84

It was very fitting that Tom Collett should follow Stanley Wells. The two of them had joined in 1949. Tom had begun with the soubriquet Mr Wardle, which passed to Stanley Wells in 1958 when Tom became Lieutenant Tappleton (Dr Slammer's Second). When Tom Collett took over as the sixth Mr Pickwick, he was 67 and in his 24 years' membership of the City Pickwick Club had rarely missed a dinner.

From the beginning of his membership the printing firm Adams Bros and Shardlow, of which he was a director, always produced the menus and other printed materials for the City Pickwick Club.

Unfortunately rapid inflation continued throughout the sixth Mr Pickwick's tenure. All too regularly he was faced with trying to balance the books by raising the cost of subscriptions and, even more unpopularly, raising the cost of the dinner. Subscriptions rose again in 1978 and the joining fee was also raised to £5. Dinner fees fared worse. In 1975 the club found it was subsidising members' dinners to the tune of £130 on each occasion so the price rose to £7. In 1979 it went to £9, then to £10 and by 1980 it had reached £12.50. Attempts were made to reduce costs. Oysters had already gone as a starter more because of reports of digestive issues than for monetary reasons. Salmon had replaced the oysters but in 1976 smoked mackerel appeared on the menu as a cheaper option. At the same time the fine wines remained fine but slightly cheaper!

Tom Collett's days were also dominated by membership problems. It was not that the club lacked members, indeed numbers stood comfortably around 60, rather that members were not good at responding to the summons. On occasions the committee lamented the fact that whilst 24 people sent apologies, 22 never bothered to reply. Meetings at the *George and Vulture* were a little thin. Once in 1981 only 14 members gathered for dinner, but fortunately they brought 13 guests with them to bolster numbers. This increased concern about the club's survival. Set against that, some members were exceeding loyal. In 1977 Lennard Hearn and K R Herring were the first men to record 50 years' membership of the City Pickwick Club, a feat which took them back to the days of the founder, James Roll.

Wardle and his Friends Under the Influence of the "Salmon"

Although membership issues challenged the club it was in many ways an exciting time. The club was delighted to welcome Cedric Dickens, great-grandson of the novelist, as a member in October 1975, introduced by Whiffin (Maurice Cocking). Members of the Dickens family did come to some events, but it was 20 years since any of them had been a member of the club, so the arrival of Joseph Smiggers was a delight.

With Joseph Smiggers came the club tie at a cost of £5.50 to members. There had been two decades of committee deliberations about the possibility of members having Pickwick waistcoats or club waistcoat buttons but no decision was ever reached. Cedric not only suggested the club tie, but was prepared to organise its manufacture and distribution. Later it became the custom for new members to receive the club tie when Augustus Snodgrass wrote to welcome them into membership. 'Tradition demands that this should be worn at all club functions,' he informed new members, warning, 'Defaulters are liable to be fined!'

In 1974 the Pickwick Club of Cape Town was in the process of being set up and their honorary secretary wrote to his opposite number at the City Pickwick Club seeking advice on procedures from the London branch. The following year one of the Cape Town members on business in London made contact with the club and was delighted to learn the City Pickwick Club wanted to be affiliated to their brethren in Cape Town. Pickwickian hospitality was reciprocated in 1981 when members from the City Pickwick Club dined at the Pickwick Tavern in Cape Town.

In an attempt to improve attendance figures at dinners, various suggestions were made about rescheduling meetings. Moving the February dinner into April or May was considered and rejected, but it was thought transferring the November meeting into early December would be more convenient for members. So the pattern of February, March, October and December dinners was settled in Tom Collett's time.

Poor health caused the sixth Mr Pickwick to miss meetings and in 1984 he decided to resign. He nominated Murray Fox as the seventh Mr Pickwick, a decision that was warmly approved by members.

The Seventh Mr Pickwick

Sir Murray Fox *represented the Ward of Cripplegate Within on Common Council, was Alderman of the Ward of Bread Street and had been Master of the Wheelwrights' Company. He served as Lord Mayor in 1974.*

Sir Henry Murray Fox GBE, MA, FRICS – Mr Pickwick 1984–99

Murray Fox's time as Mr Pickwick was dominated from the outset by uncertainties about the survival of the *George and Vulture*. For most of the time the City Pickwick Club had been meeting at the hostelry there had been rumours about it being closed down.

In 1984 the club was informed that the lease on the *George and Vulture* would expire at the end of that year and rebuilding was scheduled to take place. 'The sword of Damocles hangs over our beloved hostelry,' Augustus Snodgrass noted in the minutes of a committee meeting. Talk of the *George and Vulture* being turned into a pub downstairs threw the Club into a turmoil and committee members began searching for other possible dinner venues. In the event the club continued dining there for a further ten years, always being told by the management, who were operating on a month-by-month basis, that each meeting was likely to be their last. In fact it was October 1994 before the City Pickwick Club found itself homeless. Their two autumn dinners that year were taken at the restaurant in Bleeding Heart Yard, a suitable choice, the committee felt, in view of its convenience and mention in *Little Dorrit*. However they were in total agreement that the service was not as good as they been used to at the *George and Vulture*, where Ray Hall looked after them well.

One good thing to come out of the club's temporary move was that in March 1994, when it was known this would be the City Pickwick Club's final dinner at the *George and Vulture* for a while, commemorative photographs were taken.

During these turbulent times, the City Pickwick Club's memorabilia were lodged in various places for safe-keeping. Some went to Guildhall library and others were looked after by members. As so often happens in situations like this, items became lost, some were damaged and people couldn't remember who was looking after what, so some interesting memorabilia vanished.

After a few months out of the *George and Vulture,* manager Ray Hall said he was permitted to accept bookings on a week-by-week basis. The City Pickwick Club gratefully took their chance and dinners resumed at the correct place in the spring of 1995. Although plans to 'remodel' the ancient hostelry that summer were still being talked about, the club was home again.

Commemorative photographs of the City Pickwick Club's 'last' dinner at the George and Vulture *were taken in March 1994. There was great uncertainty at the time about whether the club would be able to return to its historic venue.*

A Hundred Years of the City Pickwick Club

Pickwickians, March 1994.

Opposite: The City Pickwick Club in 1998. Front row (l to r): Philip Potter (Mr Blotton), John Heffernan (Mr Skimpin), Sir Murray Fox (Mr Pickwick GC, MPC), Douglas Woodward (Alfred Jingle), Ivan Nellist (Hunt), Derek Kemp (Mr Jackson). Second row (l to r): Ian McNeil (Augustus Snodgrass), ?, Joe Brown (Mr Smouch), George Challis (Mr Mallard), Nigel Kemp (Mr Podder), Cedric Dickens (Joseph Smiggers PVP, MPC), Geoffrey Stallworthy (Mr Jinks), John Taylor (Mr Namby), Robert Hamblin (Hon Mr Crushton). Third row (l to r): ?, ?, Frank Steiner (Nathaniel Pipkin), Michael Beale (Rev. Stiggins), Sir Peter Gadsden (Brother Tadger), Peter Fox (Peter Magnus), Godfrey Jacobs (Mr Wicks), Sir Anthony Driver (Tony Weller), Maurice Cocking (Whiffin). Fourth Row (l to r): Tom Wilmot (Mr Pott), Michael Snyder (Mr Mivins), Sir Brian Jenkins (Jack Bamber), Sir John Chalstrey (Benjamin Allen), Richard Agutter (Hon Samuel Slumkey). Fifth row (l to r): Andrew Skinner (Mr Lowten), Clive Martin (Col Bulder), Robert Shillingford (Joe), John Holland (Bob Sawyer), ? , John Clarke (Mr Grundy), David Shalit (Hon Wilmot Snipe), John Haynes (Tom Roker), Roger Barnes (Mr Perker). Sixth row (l to r): Vincent Emms (Mr Raddle), Brian Boreham (Mr Trundle), Sir Anthony Grant (Sir Thomas Clubber), John Williams (Serjeant Buzfuz), Clifford Newbold (Daniel Grummer), ?, Anthony Howlett (Mr Dumkins), Colin Parsons (Mr Muzzle).

It was unfortunate that Murray Fox's period of office was such a difficult one. Perhaps it was because of the uncertainties about their future meetings that caused members to be lax about attending. Numbers at the dinners hovered between 20 and 30, but on one occasion fell as low as 18. Discussions about rescheduling dinners began again. Should the December meeting move forward to late November and the March dinner move to the end of the month?

It is not surprising that attempts to generate interest in a Ladies' Evening floundered. The idea was first mooted in 1984 when it was suggested that a Ladies' Night, held at the Farmers' and Fletchers' Hall, would be an excellent way to mark the City Pickwick Club's 75th anniversary. Discussions about including ladies at one event in the year rumbled on for another decade without any great enthusiasm. Objections were raised about the cost of such an event and the formality it would impose. Another member said the aims of the club did not translate well out of its traditional dinner and toast format. In 1990 a visit to Chatham was organised with the ladies in mind but when only three people signed up, the event was cancelled.

In 1995 Murray Fox told the committee he was thinking of retiring as Mr Pickwick because he had been in office since 1983, but he promised to give them two years' notice. In the event he continued as Mr Pickwick until March 1999 when he was presented with a silver salver and framed declaration of thanks for his hard work. He passed away in November of that year at the age of 87. Murray Fox had led the City Pickwick Club through the most difficult time in its history, but managed to keep them together and still established at the *George and Vulture*.

The Eighth Mr Pickwick

Sir Peter Gadsden *came from a mineral trading background and had served the City well in many offices, culminating in Lord Mayor in 1979–80.*

Sir Peter Gadsden GBE, AC, FREng – Mr Pickwick
1999–2006

Sir Peter Gadsden joined the City Pickwick Club in 1961 and had loyally attended dinners ever since, only missing them if he was abroad on business. He believed in the importance of the City Pickwick Club and was concerned that it was struggling to survive. One of the first things he did on taking office was to ensure that proper records were kept. The new Augustus Snodgrass who took office at the same time in March 1999 had forms designed for those seeking membership. At Mr Pickwick's suggestion, the age of those seeking membership was to be included and, more significantly, nominees had to commit to attending the club twice a year. As one who ran a tight ship, Sir Peter insisted that proper minutes of meetings be kept. Guest speakers were asked to deposit a copy of their speech in the club archive and Mr Pickwick began the tradition of giving a brief but concise report of the previous year's activities at the club's meeting in March.

The financial affairs of the club were scrutinised and member's standing orders were sorted out. It transpired that members were paying varying amounts depending on when they had joined. By the autumn of 1999 members were all required to pay £10 annual subscription and it cost £10 to join. Proper audited accounts came in and members who neglected to respond to letters to upgrade their subscription were eventually deemed to have resigned membership.

Believing that the membership was the club's life blood, Sir Peter set about making membership of the City Pickwick Club something worth striving for. He noted that 'recent attendance levels were not satisfactory and needed to be rebuilt'. Only 17 members attended the dinner at the start of 1999, but fortunately they brought the same number of guests. Only 23 apologies were received. Within a month of Mr Pickwick's new campaign to boost membership, 'Mr Snodgrass reported a record attendance for the dinner'. Members who didn't attend regularly or didn't pay their fees received letters inviting them to put things right and, if there was still no response after a few months, their membership was revoked.

Mr Pickwick set out to make membership of the City Pickwick Club prestigious. Club rules had set the membership number at 60 but it was decided to raise this to 83 members and maintain an official waiting list of applicants. The *George and Vulture* could

Headquarters —
THE GEORGE & VULTURE,
ST. MICHAEL'S ALLEY. E.C.3.

78, RUSSELL COURT,

RUSSELL SQUARE,

W.C. 1.

TEL. TERMINUS 2132

....19

Dear Sir,

       Kindly let me have a remittance as per account below, and oblige.

       Yours faithfully,

FRANK G. CARPENTER,

Hon. Sec.

Entrance fee   ...   .   :   :

Subscriptions <u>due in advance</u>

     to March, 19............ ...   ...   :   :

                         :   :

                         :   :

                 £   :   :

A form from the 1930s requesting members to pay their subscription.

only accommodate 55 diners and that was quite cramped. In fact in November 2000 the committee decided to cap the number of diners at 46 to ensure sufficient space for members and guests to circulate during 'wanities'.

Sir Peter also recommended the club balance its books better. A close look at the accounts revealed that diners were still being subsidised, so in January 2001 the cost of the dinner went up to £30 for members and £36.50 for guests, who were also presented with a copy of *Pickwick Papers*. The annual membership fee was £25 and in 2002 the joining fee rose to £105. Not only could the club pay its way comfortably now, but it had adequate funds to add an annual donation to the Charles Dickens Museum in addition to the Lord Mayor's charity.

One of the changes instituted by Mr Pickwick was that meetings were kept to strict times. A quarter of an hour was shaved off the dinner so members could leave at 8.30 pm promptly and catch their train home. This was achieved by reducing the speeches. It had become customary for there to be two guest speakers. One would propose the Immortal Memory and the other would reply for the guests. The reply for the guests was reduced to two or

Permit me, Sir, to invite you in the name of Mr. Pickwick, and his brother members of the Club which derives its name from him to partake of a snug little dinner at the George and Vulture Tavern and Hotel, George Yard, Lombard Street, City, on Monday,   at 6·15 p.m. precisely.

You may confidently expect to have the gratification of meeting a number of those who have rendered themselves celebrated by their Works and Talents.

Your obedient Servant,

Augustus Snodgrass
Honorary Secretary
of the City Pickwick Club.

The George and Vulture.

Coaches and Chairs ~ 8·45 p.m.
"Feasts of Reason and Flows of Soul"

three minutes and guests' welcome was similarly shortened to one line.

Mr Pickwick thought the menu was too heavy and so he set about changing to a lighter one. The oxtail soup was dropped in favour of smoked salmon. The soup had been dropped in 1998 at the height of the BSE scare when the minutes noted: 'All those present appreciated the problems, however stupid.' Instead starters called 'The President's Special' appeared, as did 'London Particular'. Various alternative main courses were tried, but members objected and so the Pickwick pie with seasonal vegetables was reinstated. A lighter sweet course did come in, often it was a fresh fruit salad, but it appeared on the menu with intriguing names like 'Jingle's Treat', 'Mary Weller's trifle' and 'Smigger's favourite'. By popular demand, the whole 'Dingley Dell stilton' remained a fixture.

At the same time as these menu changes were being sampled, charges for the dinner were revised. The new dining fee of £40 included pre-dinner drinks rather than requiring everyone to queue and pay at the bar. There were some objections from people who did not drink but it was soon accepted as a more civilised arrangement.

Under the new Mr Pickwick, committee meetings ran like clockwork and the dinners attracted a full turnout. It soon became essential for members intending to dine at the *George and Vulture* to accept the summons as soon as it arrived or there would be no space for them.

The taxing subject of a Ladies' Dinner was raised in January 2000 and Mr Pickwick gave it his whole-hearted support. The first Ladies' Dinner was held at the *George and Vulture* in June 2000. There were tickets for 42 diners and these were immediately snapped up.

Following on from the success of the Ladies' Dinner a coach trip to Rochester was proposed in the summer and plans for another Ladies' Dinner began. This time it was felt the *George and Vulture* would be too small and so the Athenaeum, famed for its Dickens connection, was favoured. In his review of 2002, Mr Pickwick remarked on the way in which the Ladies' Dinner had sold out within days and a waiting list had been started. 'The measure of success of any Club must be in the strength of its membership,' Sir Peter said. 'The fact we are at our permitted maximum (90) and have an ever increasing waiting list does, I think, speak for itself.'

The first Ladies' Dinner was held at the George and Vulture *on 12 June 2000. All tickets sold out within days of being offered.*

The following year he reported: 'The popularity of the Club is such that there is now a very long waiting list of gentlemen who wish to join our number. Whilst this is more than encouraging, it does in turn present its own problems. It may well be that we shall have to declare the membership "closed" until such time as those on our waiting list have been accommodated.'

The success of the City Pickwick Club now seemed assured. Once again the Ladies' Dinner, held in the summer of 2004, sold out instantly and the waiting list for tickets grew longer and longer. Plans for a future dinner at which ladies were guests focused around 'Cedric at 90', the planned celebration of Cedric Dickens' birthday in June 2006. Sadly, on 11th February of that year, Cedric died

only a few months short of his 90th birthday. As the last of Charles Dickens' great-grandsons and a loyal member of the City Pickwick Club for over 30 years, Cedric's loss was keenly felt. Knowing how much he enjoyed a party, it was decided to continue with the plans for a June celebration to which ladies were invited, but change it into a party to celebrate his remarkable life. The event held at the Army & Navy Club, 'in some style' it was reported, was immensely popular with 80 members and guests remembering Cedric in the way he would have wanted. A fund was set up to purchase a memorial bench for 48 Doughty Street in Cedric's memory and to present it to the Charles Dickens Museum. The location was chosen because it was at 48 Doughty Street that Dickens had written the final six parts of *Pickwick Papers*. The bench was placed in the garden on the 136th anniversary of Charles Dickens' death.

In 2006 the committee decided it was an appropriate time to reintroduce honorary membership for 'the small number of people who Mr Pickwick felt should be rewarded by the club' because it was considered this was 'the only way to show appreciation in a meaningful way'. Honorary membership, which had been regularly discussed in the past, had been given to Sir Harry Secombe 40 years earlier in gratitude for his kindness and generosity to the City Pickwick Club. In 2006 Sam Weller (Christopher Giles) was honoured in this way 'for all the good work he had done as secretary'. Lord Wedgwood and John Mohin were made honorary members in recognition of 'what they had so very generously and altruistically given to the club' and George Stylianou of the *George and Vulture* 'for his enthusiasm for all things Dickensian and the way we are looked after here at the *George and Vulture,* which is "above and beyond the call of duty"'.

When members of the City Pickwick Club met for their first meeting in January 2007, it was under the aegis of a new Mr Pickwick. Sir John Chalstrey asked members to stand in silence to remember the loss of two of their members who died on the same day in December. John Williams had served the club well as Serjeant Buzfuz since 1994 and taken an active part in research and plans for the publication of this centenary history. Also on 4th December, Mr Pickwick, Sir Peter Gadsden, died suddenly at his home in Shropshire. Sir Peter was the longest serving member of the City Pickwick Club, having been elected in March 1961. Not only had he attended dinners regularly, but he had taken a very active part in revitalising the City Pickwick Club by introducing new members and eminent guests to the *George and Vulture.* 'The supreme networker', Brother Tadger called Sir Peter in the speech given to the Immortal Memory of Charles Dickens. The strong position in which the club finds itself 100 years after its formation owes much to the contributions of the eighth Mr Pickwick.

The Ninth Mr Pickwick

Sir John Chalstrey *was an eminent surgeon at St Bartholomew's Hospital until his retirement, Alderman of Vintry Ward and Lord Mayor of London in 1995.*

Sir John Chalstrey MA, MD, DSc, FRCS – Mr Pickwick 2006–

With the soubriquet Benjamin Allen, Sir John Chalstrey became a member of the City Pickwick Club in February 1987. Twenty years later he found himself unexpectedly picking up the mantle of the ninth Mr Pickwick. At the same time His Honour Judge Brian Barker, the Common Serjeant of London, was elected as Serjeant Buzfuz. With the City Pickwick Club once again in good hands, business resumed. High on Mr Pickwick's agenda were plans for the forthcoming centenary of the club. This history, known affectionately as 'the book', was already well in hand and Pickwickians were delighted when the senior Alderman below the chair, Ian Luder (Tom Wildspark) agreed to Mr Pickwick's request that the Centenary Dinner be held at Mansion House. The same delight was also expressed when the Duke of Gloucester accepted the invitation to give the Toast to the Immortal Memory.

Links with similar organisations continue to thrive. The City Pickwick Club responded positively to the Charles Dickens Museum's request for members to assist them in their centenary plans. Meetings also began with the three twenty-first century Pickwick Clubs 'to explore whether there would be ways of co-operating with each other for *mutual benefit*', and once again there were discussions about changing the menu.

In the Centenary Year the City Pickwick Club is thriving, with a strong and enthusiastic membership that would have gladdened the heart of its founder, Sir James Roll.

The Headquarters of the City Pickwick Club
The *George and Vulture*, St. Michael's Alley, Cornhill

To speak of the City Pickwick Club immediately conjures up the vision of a convivial evening at the *George and Vulture*. It is a hundred years since James Roll, the first Mr Pickwick, chose the *George and Vulture* for the City Pickwick Club's inaugural dinner on 16th March 1909. Since then the club has wined, dined and socialised there four times a year – barring a few closures for renovations and world wars.

The GEORGE & VULTURE

St. Michaels Alley, Cornhill,

London. E.C.3

A sketch of the George and Vulture *showing it in the first half of the twentieth century.*

It comes as no surprise to learn the *George and Vulture* was already favoured by Dickens' connoisseurs long before James Roll chose to base the City Pickwick Club there. Indeed his Pickwick Coaching Club used to include a visit to the ancient chop house as part of their Pickwick itinerary, although it is not recorded how adept Alderman Roll was at negotiating the narrow passageways of George Yard with his coach and four!

It is not known when Dickens first acquainted himself with the *George and Vulture* but it was undoubtedly a favourite with him. In 1836 he wrote:

> There still remain some old inns, which have preserved their external features unchanged, and which have escaped alike the rage for public improvement, and the encroachment of private speculation.

A receipt in the possession of the late Cedric Dickens relates to one very significant visit Dickens made to the hostelry. The bill, dated 20th January 1837, indicates that the novelist spent £11 entertaining 34 friends handsomely to a meal with wine and cigars. This has echoes of the first appearance of the *George and Vulture* in *Pickwick Papers*. On that occasion Mr Pickwick awakes late on Christmas Eve morning with 'a confused recollection of having, severally and confidentially, invited somewhere

about five-and-forty people to dine with him at the George and Vulture, the very first time they came to London'.

From then on, the *George and Vulture* appears regularly in the book because Dickens ensured 'Mr Pickwick and Sam took up their present abode in very good, old-fashioned, and comfortable quarters: to wit, the George and Vulture Tavern and Hotel, George Yard, Lombard Street'.

This tavern and hotel remains Mr Pickwick's base throughout the novel until he finally retires to Dulwich at the end of *Pickwick Papers*. A few noteworthy episodes occur during Pickwick's sojourn there. There is the occasion when Mr Jackson, senior clerk to Messrs Dodson and Fogg, is sent to the *George and Vulture* to subpoena Pickwick's three friends and Sam Weller to attend court in the case of Bardell v. Pickwick. Indeed poor Pickwick himself, although in bed in his room at the hostelry, is arrested there and taken to the Fleet prison. Fortunately justice prevails and on his release Mr Pickwick returns to his abode in George Yard.

Throughout the novel, the famous hostelry is backdrop to several domestic cameos. There is the occasion Mr Winkle brings his new wife Arabella to meet Pickwick. Later the same young lady

A scene in the George and Vulture *when Mr and Mrs Winkle call on Mr Pickwick to acquaint him with their marriage.*

has a more unpleasant encounter at the *George and Vulture* when Mr Winkle senior turns up to view his new daughter-in-law. All ends happily when he finally pronounces her 'a charming little daughter-in-law after all'.

The other drama Dickens sets at the *George and Vulture* is when Sam Weller retires to one of the window seats at the inn to read a letter from his father, ably assisted by the pretty house-maid Mary. All of these provided ample scope for Dickens' illustrators who were familiar with the hostelry, but it is difficult to be sure how authentic the background to these scenes is.

The real-life *George and Vulture* dates back hundreds of years before Dickens. There are twelfth-century references to a lodging house called the George on the site. Two hundred years later this place acquired a Vulture in its name, possibly because it became linked to St George and the dragon. It is known that dragons were sometimes portrayed as vultures in pictures, which is not surprising given the problems artists had in locating suitable material to copy. At other times in its history the ancient chop house was called Dolly's and then Thomas's Chop House, but the old name

Phiz captures a scene set in the George and Vulture.

reasserted itself in the seventeenth century and has remained ever since.

Although the site has remained unchanged, the building certainly has not. Two former inns on the site burned down. The Great Fire of London in 1666 removed the chop house Pepys knew, and its replacement was reduced to ashes in 1748. Even the hostelry Dickens had in mind when he wrote *Pickwick Papers* is not quite the same. During the 1850s and again in the 1880s, the building was altered and partly rebuilt. Since then, as City Pickwick Club members know all too well, there have been numerous attempts at remodelling the ancient hostelry which, on occasion, have caused the club to go elsewhere for brief periods.

Despite various new owners and attempts to make changes, the *George and Vulture* has remained the established and much loved headquarters of the City Pickwick Club.

Whiffin, Town Crier of Eatanswill, 42 years a City Pickwickian and with the longest continuous membership, puts quill to paper to capture the essence of a convivial evening there:

The President's silver gilt and enamel badge of office was presented to the Club in 1959 by the fourth Mr Pickwick, Sir Frederick Rowland. His successor, Major Stanley Wells, had it inscribed in 1972.

A convivial evening at the George & Vulture *with the Ladies.*

⤳ B ⤳

It has not been unknown for President Mr Pickwick to re-enact this scene at dinners of the Club!

The eighth Mr Pickwick, Sir Peter Gadsden, was responsible for bringing the much-discussed Ladies Night to fruition, presides at the second Ladies Night on 9th June 2003.

⤳ C ⤳

Ladies Night.

From the Club's archives emerge this genial Mr Pickwick and his comely escort. Sadly their names are lost in the Swirl of Time. It is advised that all enquiries should be addressed to the Pickwickians' Permanent Retirement Home, Dingley Dell c/o Mr Wardle.

⮜ D ⮞

The Headquarters of the City Pickwick Club

When the winds gust and the rain spatters City pavements and it is night, they come: they bend their path from towns, villages and hamlets that lie to the north, south, west and east of the great City which has the George & Vulture at its heart.

They are the Pickwickians. They present in a variety of age, shape and assortment. One purpose they all have in common: 'A snug little dinner' with each happy other in the benevolent presence of their revered leader, Samuel Pickwick Esq. GCMPC (General Chairman-Member Pickwick Club).

For a hundred years, generation after generation of Club members have wended way to its antique, frosted-glass doors bearing still the legend: 'Fosters Chop House'. Observe, too, the huge polished brass plaques upon brick each side. A searching eye will discern the last embedded trace of 'Fosters' all but obliterated by the assiduity of polishers long since left to polish plaques in Paradise.

Through the yielding doors one arrives upon a scene of Victorian cosiness. Long tables, short tables, cubicled tables, all graced by starch-white table linen; cutlery set as smart as Lancers, glasses as upstanding as bright-eyed Grenadiers anticipating their first delivery of grape! See, there, at the top table set out for Mr Pickwick, the garlanded bust of Charles Dickens, the table prepared for Pickwick's guests and for his principal guest who will later rise to the occasion, praise Charles Dickens to the rim and invite all Pickwickians to stand and toast 'The Immortal Memory of Charles Dickens'. But that is not yet.

The bust of Charles Dickens is set on the top table at every dinner.

First, there is the happy hubbub of Pickwickians and their guests arriving in party spirit. Indeed, the very next step is to cut a path through the effervescence of bonhomie to the crowded bar. Libation in hand, members then ascend the creaking spiral staircase to the floor above where already Mr Pickwick is ensconced to conduct 'Transactions'. The hurly-burly of wit, humour, comment (often shouted), questions ('how much is in the kitty?'), all in the serious business of running the most erudite, rumbustious club in the whole Square Mile and probably in the entire United Kingdom, Colonies and Commonwealth.

Transactions done and dusted, it's down the creaking spiral, once more unto the bar, dear friends, where glasses are recharged in token of humanity, health and future prosperity!

Word arrives from the subterranean kitchen that the Pickwick Pie is on the bubble, that all is ready and will Whiffin ring his bell! Whiffin's Great Bell rings out a concerto to rival the combined clanging of a dozen assorted fire engines racing to quench the Great Fire.

'Wittels, Gentlemen, Wittels ... please!'

All respond 'Muffins!' as, indeed did that odd inspired Eatanswillian in Chapter 13!

Seated all, Mr Pickwick now requires the said Whiffin to deliver his own home-baked Grace, a simple plea to the Great Master Chef:

Lord,

May it be Thy will

To bless our Eatanswill.

Amen.

Then without further ado, the chosen Chairman for the soirée bangs his commanding gavel, calling upon the Hon Secretary Augustus Snodgrass 'to bring in the Pickwick Papers ...'

Dear Reader, let the industrious, detailed delineations of Augustus Snodgrass himself transport you through the banquet that awaits, the banter that four times a year suffuses with happiness the welcoming walls of that good old hostelry, that temple of temperance and hospitality, the George & Vulture, George Yard, City.

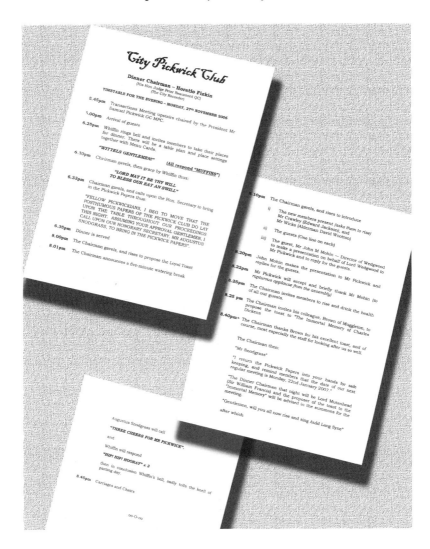

City Pickwick Club

Dinner Chairman – Horatio Fizkin
(His Hon Judge Peter Beaumont QC)
(The City Recorder)

TIMETABLE FOR THE EVENING – MONDAY, 27ᵗʰ NOVEMBER 2006

5.45pm Transactions Meeting upstairs chaired by the President Mr Samuel Pickwick GC MPC.

7.00pm Arrival of guests

6.25pm Whiffin rings bell and invites members to take their places for dinner. There will be a table plan and place settings together with Menu Cards.

"WITTELS GENTLEMEN!" (All respond *"MUFFINS"*)

6.30pm Chairman gavels, then grace by Whiffin thus:

"LORD MAY IT BE THY WILL TO BLESS OUR EAT AN SWILL"

6.33pm Chairman gavels, and calls upon the Hon. Secretary to bring in the Pickwick Papers thus:

"FELLOW PICKWICKIANS, I BEG TO MOVE THAT THE POSTHUMOUS PAPERS OF THE PICKWICK CLUB DO LAY UPON THE TABLE THROUGHOUT OUR PROCEEDINGS THIS NIGHT. ASSUMING YOUR APPROVAL GENTLEMEN, I CALL UPON OUR HONORARY SECRETARY, MR AUGUSTUS SNODGRASS, TO BRING IN THE PICKWICK PAPERS"

6.35pm Dinner is served

8.00pm The Chairman gavels, and rises to propose the Loyal Toast

8.01pm The Chairman announces a five-minute watering break

8.10pm The Chairman gavels, and rises to introduce

i) The new members present *(asks them to rise)*
Mr Crawley (Edward Jackson), and
Mr Wicks (Alderman David Wootton)

ii) The guests (One line on each)

iii) The guest, Mr John M Mohin – Director of Wedgwood to make a presentation on behalf of Lord Wedgwood to Mr Pickwick and to reply for the guests.

8.20pm John Mohin makes the presentation to Mr Pickwick and replies for the guests.

8.22pm Mr Pickwick will accept and briefly thank Mr Mohin (to rapturous applause from the assembly)

8.25pm The Chairman invites members to rise and drink the health of all our guests.

8.25 pm The Chairman invites his colleague, Brown of Muggleton, to propose the toast to 'The Immortal Memory of Charles Dickens'

8.40pm* The Chairman thanks Brown for his excellent toast, and of course, most especially the staff for looking after us so well.

The Chairman then:

"Mr Snodgrass"

"I return the Pickwick Papers into your hands for safe keeping, and remind members that the date of our next regular meeting is Monday. 22nd January 2007."

"The Dinner Chairman that night will be Lord Mutanhead (Sir William Francis) and the proposer of the toast to the 'Immortal Memory' will be advised in the summons for the meeting.

"Gentlemen, will you all now rise and sing Auld Lang Syne"

after which

Augustus Snodgrass will call

"THREE CHEERS FOR MR PICKWICK".

and

Whiffin will respond

"HIP! HIP! HOORAY" x 3

then in conclusion Whiffin's bell, sadly tolls the knell of parting day.

8.45pm Carriages and Chairs

∞-0-∞

At the conclusion of the evening's proceedings, and after Auld Lang Syne has been sung, Whiffin responds to Snodgrass who calls for 'Three Cheers for Mr Pickwick!'; Whiffin leads a club 'Hip! Hip! Hurray!' three times. As the clamour dies, Whiffin upon a sad, almost disconsolate slow note sounds a wistful knell for the departing Pickwickians.
Exeunt all.

Whiffin (left), the longest serving member of the City Pickwick Club, with Cedric Dickens (right), great-grandson of Charles Dickens. Whiffin proposed Cedric for membership of the City Pickwick Club in 1975.

The Wherefore of Whiffin

City journalist Maurice D Cocking, dubbed Whiffin, the fat crier of Eatanswill, became a member of the City Pickwick Club in October 1967, which makes him the longest serving member.

For 42 years Whiffin has played a central ceremonial role at the Pickwick dinners. Upon hearing that he was to be baptised Whiffin, crier of Eatanswill, he searched the antique shops of Tunbridge Wells and purchased a large handbell for £5. At his first ever Pickwick dinner in October 1967 he gave a vigorous demonstration of the bell's power and clarity.

After many years' enthusiastic service, the original Tunbridge bell was lost in a taxicab and never found. Considerable research by Mrs Whiffin discovered a second bell for a never-yet disclosed sum, a nineteenth-century school bell which had belonged to the headmistress of a Hereford school. It is this bell of pure and perfect pitch which now rings in the ears of all participating Pickwickians.

Some Other Pickwick Clubs

The Pickwick Bicycle Club

The club was formed on 22nd June 1870 when six cycling enthusiasts met at the Downs Hotel, Hackney Downs, East London, and decided to form themselves into a bicycle club. As the formation coincided with the death of Charles Dickens, the name 'Pickwick' was chosen in honour of the novelist. From that time onwards the club has an unbroken history as an active cycling organisation and in the worthwhile task of spreading fellowship and conviviality. The club is not only the oldest cycling club in the world but also the oldest Dickensian association still in existence.

The club currently has 186 members. The membership is limited to 208 plus retired members (which were 14 in 2009), the limit set by the number of male characters or identifiable individuals in *Pickwick Papers*. Each member on election is given the soubriquet of a character and is addressed as such at club functions. The annual president is addressed as Samuel Pickwick during his term of office. Whilst maintaining its cycling connections with an annual ride in Hampton Court Park, joining other veteran cycle clubs at an annual meeting in Oxfordshire and riding through the Hertfordshire countryside on a day in June, the club meet twice a year for lunch. At the President's Luncheon held on the first Thursday in May about 450 members and guests enjoy a hearty meal, with nearly 600 meeting in December for the Annual Garden Party. Entertainment is provided and traditions involving trumpeters from the Lifeguards and Chelsea pensioners are regularly included.

In 1986 Cedric Dickens was elected an honorary member and remained such until his death. His grandson Ian Dickens continues the family connection with the soubriquet Boz.

The Dickens Pickwick Club

The club was formed in 1976 following 25 years of dinners organised through Cedric Dickens' employer. Cedric retired that year but wanted to continue the dinners so he became president. There is an annual dinner in December at the *George and Vulture*, including a toast to the Immortal Memory, and members assume Pickwickian names. The annual dinners are well attended and continue to be popular in the twenty-first century.

The Pickwick Club, London

Founded in 1971 by four members of the insurance community in the City, two from Royal Insurance, one from Ormond Jones and Co, loss adjusters, and another, an insurance broker. The club meets for luncheon four times a year (including St George's Day and Trafalgar Day). In its earlier days the club enjoyed excellent meetings at a series of well-known watering-holes including the Cheshire Cheese, Fleet Street, the City Livery Club, the Law Society, the Waldorf Hotel, the Wig and Pen Club, the Royal Thames Yacht Club, but now has just two 'home bases': the Farmers' Club in Whitehall Court and the George in Borough High Street.

Every club member is paired with another member, and they are jointly responsible for organising the lunch programme on a particular day. There is no permanent or annually elected chairman. The duty to host comes round broadly every two or three years. The joint-hosts are responsible for everything: booking the venue, the menu, wines and selecting entertainment and inviting a speaker. Although tradition dictates the very broad format of each lunch, joint-hosts have a wide discretion as to how to make a lunch enjoyable and different.

All members have Pickwickian names but the founders had unanimously agreed that the nom de plume 'Mr Pickwick' should never be allocated 'because no one member should ever be considered that special'.

Total membership in the earlier days was deliberately restricted but current membership is maintained at around 30 members.

The Sidmouth Pickwick Club

The Sidmouth Pickwick Club was launched on 7th March 2008 with Derek Davies – Mr Pickwick – elected as General Chairman; Mr Henry Dickens Hawksley CBE became Perpetual Vice-President with the soubriquet Joseph Smiggers PVP MPC. Mrs Jane Monk (née Dickens) became an honorary member with the soubriquet Lady Clubber.

Appendix 1
Founder Members in 1909

From the minute book

On **Tuesday 16th February 1909** at a dinner given by Mr James Roll, CC, at the George and Vulture, St Michael's Alley, Cornhill, EC, it was decided to form a club of not more than 30 members, the idea being the association of the George and Vulture Tavern and Charles Dickens.

The following gentlemen agreed to be members:

James Roll (Director Pearl Assurance Ltd)	Adelaide Place, London Bridge, EC
Chance Newton (Journalist)	The Referee, Tudor Street, EC
C Webster	Cambridge Park, Wanstead
A E Binstead	The Sporting Times, Fleet Street, E
G Bate	35 Bedford Row, WC
H A Summer	Southern Hey, Loughton
W Baxter	79½ Gracechurch Street, EC
T J Cox	5 Venner Road, Sydenham
J B Willis	13 Devonshire Square, EC
J T Gardner	The George and Vulture Tavern, EC
John Sulley	46 Cannon Street, EC
F Newman	50a Southerland Square, Walworth, SE
F D Bowles CC	Adelaide Place, London Bridge, EC
M R Sewell	4 Castle Court, EC
Deputy Miller-Wilkinson	St Michael's Alley, EC
J T Dormer	Albury House, Alborough Hatch, Ilford, Essex
W G Brown	8 Northstead Road, Tulse Hill, SW
A A Robinson	103 Bow Road, E

C J Smith	5 Fenchurch Street, EC
E Burford	The Chestnuts, Strawberry Hill, Teddington
G A Godfrey	4 & 5 West Smithfield, EC
J Foley	Adelaide Place, London Bridge, EC
H Wye CC	3 Milk Street, EC
R A Kearsey	4 Billiter Street, EC
H P Monckton	32 Wallbrook, EC
Charles Troup	282 Victoria Dock Road, E
G S Goodwin	70 Fairholt Road, Stamford Hill
W Rodgers	Cambridge Villas, Hainbury Road, Leytonstone
A J Dale	46 Cannon Street, EC

A month later on **Tuesday 16th March 1909** at 5.30pm the group met again to consider the name of the club.

James Roll in the Chair
Also present, Messrs Newton, Webster, Bate, Willis, Gardner, Dormer, Robinson, Burford, Godfrey, Wilkinson, Wye, Monckton, Troup, Newman and Sulley.

- Proposed by Monckton, seconded by Sulley, 'The City Pickwick Club' was carried.
- Proposed by Deputy Wilkinson, seconded by Dormer, James Roll to be President.
- Proposed by Webster, seconded by Monckton, Chance Newton to be Vice-President.
- Proposed by Willis, seconded by Gardner, H A Summer to be Hon Treasurer.
- Proposed by Robinson, seconded by Godfrey, John Sulley to be Hon Secretary.

The Rules of The City Pickwick Club

1. The Club shall be held at 'The George and Vulture', St Michael's Alley, Cornhill, EC or elsewhere as the Members shall decide, at a meeting to be called for that purpose (see also Rule 14). The Club shall not exceed 30 members.
2. A Sub-Committee shall manage the affairs of the Club

and shall consist of the President, Vice-President, three members, Hon Treasurer, Hon Secretary (three to form a quorum), with power to add to their number. The said Sub-Committee to be elected at the March meeting each year.

3. That no person be eligible to be a Member of the Club unless he shall have been proposed at one meeting, his name, address and calling announced to the Members on the notices convening the next Meeting, and he then be balloted for and elected. Two black balls to exclude.

4. There be four Meetings of the Club each year, to be held respectively on the second Monday of the months of February, March, October and November. The Annual Meeting to be in March.

5. The Dinner on all occasions to be on the table at six-thirty precisely, and the Business Meeting to be held previously.

6. That the terms of Membership of the Club shall be as follows: An entrance fee of 10 shillings and 6 pence for each new member, and an annual subscription of 10 shillings and 6 pence *payable in advance of the March Meeting.* Dinner tickets not to exceed 5 shillings each (exclusive of liquid refreshment and cigars).

7. That every member shall be at liberty to introduce one friend at each Club Dinner on payment of a sum not exceeding 5 shillings in respect of the friend so introduced (exclusive of liquid refreshment and cigars).

8. That every Member who intends to be present at the Club Dinner shall, on or before the Saturday preceding the date of the Dinner, send a written intimation to the Hon Secretary of his intention to attend, and shall state in such intimation if he intends to bring a visitor.

9. That every Member shall (if he so desire) preside as Chairman at the Club Dinner for one evening *in rotation,* and the Secretary shall issue notices accordingly, always excepting the Meeting in March, when the President is, by right of office, entitled to occupy the Chair.

10. That the funds of the Club shall be vested in the Treasurer and Secretary, and placed in the London and Joint Stocks Bank, or other approved bank, on current and deposit account.

11. Two Auditors, who shall be appointed at the February Meeting in each year, shall investigate the accounts of

the Club and report thereon at the ensuing Meeting in March.

12. If any member shall refuse to pay his subscription, when called upon by the Hon Secretary to do so, he shall be considered no longer to be a Member.

13. Every Member of the Club shall be supplied with a copy of these Rules, and by accepting such copy is deemed to have agreed to be bound thereby.

14. That none of the preceding Rules shall be varied or rescinded, nor shall any Rules be added unless written notice thereof shall have been given through the Secretary of the Club's usual notices of the Meetings, and a resolution in favour of such variation or rescission or addition to the Rules carried by a majority of three-fourths of the Members present at the next Meeting of the Club.

Notice of alteration of the Rules shall be given in writing to the Secretary fourteen days before the next Meeting.

A few notable events from the early minute book

11th October 1909 James Roll, elected Senior Sheriff of the City of London.

March 1911 Membership increased to 50.

12th February 1912 Club subscribed 5 guineas to the *Daily Telegraph* appeal for the 5 grandchildren of Charles Dickens.

November 1912 Mr Percy Fitzgerald, a personal friend of Charles Dickens, attended the Dinner and recounted his memories of the famous man.

October 1913 Membership increased to 60. Alderman Edward Cooper knighted.

8th February 1915 The Club was honoured by the presence of Henry F Dickens Esq, QC, son of Charles Dickens. A Gala evening.

October 1916 The Club heard with regret the death of the sons of Mr Henry Dickens and member William Miles, who were killed in action defending the country against 'German Kultur'. Bookcase and copies of Charles Dickens novels and other memorabilia were presented to the George and Vulture by James Roll and others.

November 1918 Donation given to Dickens Fellowship to provide books for injured soldiers. Club was visited by the Secretary of the Pickwick Bicycle Club, inviting Members to join the Bicycle Club. 43 Members accepted, 4 others were already members. H F Dickens Esq, KC elected as a member. Alderman Louis Newton knighted.

December 1919 President, Alderman James Roll, presented a silver salver to Secretary Mr C S Goodwin for his services to the Club. The Club was honoured by the presence of Mr Bransby Williams, actor, who gave a performance of his art.

March 1920 Vice-President, Sir Edward Cooper, Lord Mayor of the City of London. Captain Newton Knights MP elected member.

October 1920 Mr C H Green, Secretary of Dickens Fellowship, elected as a Member.

The President and Founder, Alderman James Roll, Lord Mayor Elect of the City of London.

> The Members of the City Pickwick Club, assembled at the George and Vulture on this first full meeting since your appointment as The Lord Mayor of London, desire to convey to you their expression of friendship and their hearty congratulations on the honour which has been conferred on you, and express the hope that you will enjoy the best of health to carry out the onerous functions which such a high office entails. And that you will be happy in the execution of those duties which we are all confident you will perform with the dignity and good feeling they demand with the real Pickwickian spirit.

14th February 1921 Death of founder member and Mine Host of the George and Vulture, Mr John Gardner.
Framed photographs of Sir Edward Cooper Bt and Alderman James Roll, hung at the George and Vulture lounge.

20th July 1921 Members of the City Pickwick Club dined at the Mansion House as guests of the President, Lord Mayor James Roll. At the event a Dickens illuminated Address and a specially bound edition of *The Posthumous Papers of the Pickwick Club* was presented to the President.

12th March 1922 The sum of 70 guineas given to the Dickens Memorial Fund, 48 Doughty Street, WC.

November 1923 Vice-President, Alderman Sir Louis Newton, Lord Mayor of the City of London.

October 1925 Death of Member Mr B W Matz, Founder of the Dickens Fellowship.

October 1926 The President purchased the Moses Pickwick Clock which was presented to the Dickens House Museum.

February 1927 Few attended the meeting due to the influenza epidemic. Death of Founder and President Sir James Roll on 30th January was reported.

March 1927 John Herbert Bishop elected President.

November 1930 Sir Henry Dickens KC and his youngest son attended the Dinner.

30th March 1936 Mr J Herbert Bishop, President of the Club, entertained members and guests at a dinner in celebration of *The Pickwick Papers*. The dinner was held at the Girdlers Hall and a full account was published in the *City Press* (3rd April 1936). The following evening many members joined in a celebration of the centenary held by the Dickens Fellowship.

3rd July1936 Death of President, Mr J H Bishop. Mr Bishop would have achieved high office in the City but for extreme poor health. Despite his infirmity he was a powerful influence in the City of London and in several Livery Companies.

FOUNDED 1909.

Headquarters:
The "George and Vulture,"
St. Michael's Alley, London, E.C.3.

MEMBERSHIP LIST 2009

Honorary Officers

President: Mr Samuel Pickwick GC MPC
(Sir John Chalstrey Kt MA MD DSc FRCS)

Vice President: Mr Joseph Smiggers PVP MPC
(Henry Dickens Hawksley CBE)

Hon. Secretary: Mr Augustus Snodgrass
(Andrew Whitton)

Hon. Treasurer: Sam No. 924
(Peter Lush FCA)

Honorary Members

LORD WEDGWOOD (November 2006)
JOHN MOHIN (November 2006)
GEORGE STYLIANOU (November 2006)
CHRISTOPHER GILES (November 2006)
Member Honoris Causa
RAVI GILL FCCA
(Mr Slasher)
September 2008

MR THOMAS ACKLAND
FCA
(Master Tommy Bardell)
February 1994

MR RICHARD AGUTTER
FCA MSI
(Hon. Samuel Slumkey)
October 1998

**MR ALDERMAN
NICHOLAS ANSTEE**
FCA
(Lieutenant Tappleton)
September 2003

**HIS HONOUR JUDGE SIR
GAVYN FARR ARTHUR**
Kt MA DCL
(Mr Whiffers)
November 2004

MR DENIS BALLARD
BA (Hons) FCA
(Captain Dowler)
November 2002

**HIS HON. JUDGE BRIAN
BARKER**
QC
The Common Serjeant of
London
(Serjeant Buzfuz)
September 2007

**MR JOHN BARKER
(Deputy)**
Chief Commoner
OBE CC
(Tom Cripps)
November 2000

MR ROGER BARNES
BA
(Mr Perker)
November 1986

MR TIMOTHY BARNES
QC
(Tom Cummins)
November 1999

MR MICHAEL BEALE
(Rev. Stiggins)
February 1989

MR SHERIFF AND ALDER-MAN MICHAEL BEAR
BSc MBA CEng MICE MStJ
(Nixon)
September 2007

HIS HONOUR JUDGE PETER BEAUMONT
QC
The Recorder of London
(Horatio Fizkin Esq)
March 2003

MR JEFFREY BINES
(Mr Bardell)
March 2005

MR GEOFFREY BOND
OBE DL
(Daniel Grummer)
September 2004

MR LESLIE BOWYER
BA (Hons) FCCA ACMA
(Mr Gunter)
November 1997

MR NIGEL BRANSON
JP
(Serjeant Snubbin)
November 2001

ALDERMAN SIR DAVID BREWER
Kt CMG
(George)
March 2006

MR NIGEL CARTWRIGHT
MBA
(Brother Mordlin)
March 2001

MR MICHAEL CASSIDY (Deputy)
CBE BA MBA
(Mr Phunky)
October 1992

MR GEORGE CHALLIS
CBE
(Mr Mallard)
October 1983

SIR JOHN CHALSTREY
Kt MA MD DSc FRCS
(Mr Samuel Pickwick)
February 1987

MR WILLIAM CHARNOCK
(Brooks)
September 2002

MR JOHN CLARKE
(Mr Podder)
November 1998

MR MAURICE COCKING
BA BSc (Econ)
(Whiffin)
October 1967

MR DENNIS COTGROVE
BA CC
(Smangle)
January 1999

SIR FREDERICK CRAWFORD
Kt DL FREng
(Mr Dodson)
September 2002

MR DEREK L DAVIES
CBE
(Angelo Cyrus Bantam)
September 2003

MR COLIN DIAPER
(Neddy)
March 2000

MR SIMON DUCKWORTH
MA DL CC
(Solomon Pell)
March 2005

DR RODNEY EDRICH
JP BA FRSA FRGS
(Mr Dumkins)
January 2005

MR GEOFFREY FINN
BCom
(Isaac)
November 2001

**MR RODNEY
FITZGERALD (Deputy)**
MBE MA
(Jack Hopkins)
January 1999

MR GRAHAM FORBES
FRICS
(Tracy Tupman)
March 2004

MR PETER FOX
MA ACII
(Mr Peter Magnus)
February 1985

MR WILLIAM FRASER
(Deputy)
OBE
(Wilkins Flasher)
October 1990

MR CHRISTOPHER GILES
FRSA FRGS
(Sam Weller)
November 1999
Honorary Member

SIR ANTHONY GRANT
Kt
(Sir Thomas Clubber)
October 1991

MR MICHAEL GRANT
(Mr Ayresleigh)
November 2004

CMDR GEORGE GREAVES
RN
(Mr Trundle)
September 2004

MR NICHOLAS HAMBLIN
BA (Hons)
(The Hon. Mr Crushton)
September 2002

DR PETER HARDWICK
QHP BSc MB FRCA CC
(Dr Payne)
March 1989

MR ANTHONY HART
OBE DSC JP FRSA FCILA
(Mr Staple)
November 1986

**HIS HON. JUDGE
RICHARD HAWKINS**
QC
(Brown of Muggleton)
September 1995

**MR HENRY DICKENS
HAWKSLEY**
CBE
(Mr Joseph Smiggers PVP
MPC)
September 2003

DR ROBERT HAWLEY
CBE DSc FREng FRSE
(Mr Blotton)
September 2002

MR JOHN HAYNES
(Tom Roker)
October 1992

MR ANDREW HEARN
ARICS
(Nathaniel Winkle)
February 1993

MR JOHN HEFFERNAN
BCom
(Mr Skimpin)
October 1989

**CAPT. CHRISTOPHER
HODGKINSON**
FRAeS FRIN FRMetS
(Mr Simpson)
September 2007

**MR JOHN HOLLAND
(Deputy)**
CBE FCA JP DL

(Bob Sawyer)
March 1998

MR PETER HORROCKS
MA FRAS
(Mr Prosee)
September 2002

MR JEREMY HYAM
BA (Hons)
(Job Trotter)
September 2006

MR GRAHAM JACKMAN
(Henry Beller)
November 2001

MR EDWARD JACKSON
(Mr Crawley)
September 2006

SIR BRIAN JENKINS
GBE MA FCA FBCS
(Jack Bamber)
February 1984

MR DEREK KEMP
CC
(Mr Jackson)
November 1981

MR DAVID LANCASTER
FCIS
(Mr Fogg)
January 2005

**ALDERMAN SIR DAVID
LEWIS**
Kt MA
(Ben Allen)
September 2007

MR PAUL LLOYD
FSI
(Frank Simmery)
January 2004

THE RT HON THE LORD MAYOR ALDERMAN IAN LUDER
BSc(Econ) FCA FTII FRSA
(Tom Wildspark)
January 2002

MR PETER LUSH
FCA
(Sam No.924)
January 2005

SIR CLIVE MARTIN
Kt OBE TD DL
(Colonel Bulder)
November 1993

MR KENNETH McALLEN
(Joe the Fat Boy)
December 1987

MR IAIN McWHIRTER
BA (Hons)
(Brother Tadger)
November 1999

MR MALCOLM MOSS
(Mr Tom Martin)
January 2001

MR JOHN NASH
(Count Smorltork)
November 1997

MR IVAN NELLIST
Dipl Arch RIBA FCIAug

MInstM
(Hunt)
October 1990

MR BRUCE NEWBIGGING
(Mr Luffey)
November 1992

ALDERMAN SIR MICHAEL OLIVER
Kt LLD DLitt DL
(Tommy)
October 1996

MR PETER OLLEY
CEng FIStructE MICE
(Pruffle)
September 2001

MR COLIN PARSONS
FCA
(Muzzle)
January 1999

MR CLAUDE PARTRIDGE
MA CPA
(Bill Stumps)
November 2000

MR ANTONY PHILLIPS
FRICS
(Thomas Burton)
November 1999

MR RICHARD PUGH
DL LLB FCA FCIS FRGS
(Mr Clarke)
September 2005

Mr GERALD PULMAN
(Deputy)
JP
(Moses Pickwick)
January 2008

MR RICHARD REGAN
(Deputy)
ACIS CC
(Mr Raddle)
September 2007

PROFESSOR DAVID RHIND
CBE FRS FBA DSc
(The Scientific Gentleman)
September 2005

MR IAN ROBERTSON
(Anthony Humm)
March 1995

MR PATRICK RONEY
(Deputy)
CBE MA
(George Nupkins)
December 1980

MR DAVID SHALIT
FCA
(Hon. Wilmot Snipe)
December 1976

MR ROBERT SHILLINGFORD
MBE MBA
(Joe)
Rejoined November 1997

MR DAVID SIMMONDS
JP BSc FRICS
(Mr Smithie)
September 2006

MR ROBERT SMITH
(Sir Geoffrey Manning)
January 2000

SIR MICHAEL SNYDER
(Deputy)
Kt FCA
(Mr Mivins)
October 1990

MR MARK SOUNDY
BA
(Leo Hunter)
February 1992

ALDERMAN SIR JOHN STUTTARD
Kt MA
(Mr Snicks)
September 2004

MR JOHN TAYLOR
TD
(Mr Namby)
November 1992

PROFESSOR MICHAEL THORNE
BSc PhD FRSA
(Crookey)
September 2005

MR LAWRENCE TURNER
OBE BSc CEng FIEE FCIBSE
(Captain Boldwig)
September 2002

MR RICHARD VARDY
FCIS ACIB MSI FRSA FRGS
(Shiny Villiam)
November 2001

MR DOUGLAS WARD
MA MSc FCGI CDipAF
FIMarEST
(Martin the Gamekeeper)
November 1999

MR ANDREW WHITTON
(Augustus Snodgrass)
March 2001

MR DAVID WICKHAM
MA FSA FRHistS
(Harris)
January 2004

BRIGADIER ROY WILDE
CBE
(Jonas Mudge)
November 2003

**MR PHILIP WILLOUGHBY
(Deputy)**
JP FCA
(Thomas Groffin)
October 1991

MR MICHAEL WILMOT
ACII
(Mr Pott)
March 2001

**MR DOUGLAS
WOODWARD**
CBE
(Alfred Jingle)
December 1987

MR NORMAN WOOLLEY
(Dr Slammer)
September 2001

**ALDERMAN DAVID
WOOTTON**
(Mr Wicks)
September 2006

Appendix 3
Subscribers to the publication of this book

The London College of
Accountancy

Master Tommy Bardell	Thomas Ackland FCA
Hon Samuel Slumkey	Richard Agutter FCA MSI
Mr Whiffers	His Hon Judge Sir Gavyn Farr
	Arthur Kt MA DCL
Captain Dowler	Denis Ballard BA (Hons) FCA
Serjeant Buzfuz	His Hon Judge Brian Barker QC
	The Common Serjeant of London
Tom Cripps	John Barker OBE CC (Deputy)
	Chief Commoner
Mr Perker	Roger A Barnes BA
Tom Cummins	Timothy Barnes QC
Rev Stiggins	Michael Beale
Nixon	Alderman Michael Bear BSc MBA
	CEng MICE
Horatio Fizkin	His Hon Judge Peter Beaumont QC
	The Recorder of London
Mr Bardell	Jeffery Bines
Daniel Grummer	Geoffrey Bond OBE DL
Serjeant Snubbin	Nigel Branson JP
George	Alderman Sir David Brewer Kt CMG
Brother Mordlin	Nigel Cartwright MBA
Mr Mallard	George Challis CBE
Mr Pickwick	Sir John Chalstrey Kt MA MD DSc
	FRCS
Brooks	William Charnock
Mr Podder	John Clarke
Whiffin	Maurice D Cocking BA BSc (Econ)
Mr Wardle	His Honour the late Michael Coombe
Mr Dodson	Sir Frederick Crawford Kt DL FREng

Angelo Cyrus Bantam	Derek Davies CBE
Neddy	Colin Diaper
Solomon Pell	Simon Duckworth MA DL CC
Mr Dumkins	Dr Rodney Edrich JP BA FRSA FRGS
Isaac	Geoffrey S Finn BCom
Jack Hopkins	Rodney FitzGerald MBE MA (Deputy)
Tracy Tupman	Graham Forbes FRICS
Peter Magnus	Peter Fox MA ACII
Lord Mutanhead	Sir William Francis (resigned)
Wilkins Flasher	William Fraser OBE (Deputy)
Samuel Pickwick	The late Sir Peter Gadsden GBE AC FREng
Sam Weller	Christopher Giles FRSA FRGS
Mr Slasher	Ravi Gill FCCA
Sir Thomas Clubber	Sir Anthony Grant Kt
Mr Trundle	Cmdr George Greaves RN
The Hon Mr Crushton	Nicholas Hamblin BA (Hons)
Mr Staple	Anthony Hart OBE DSC JP FRSA FCILA
Brown	His Hon Judge Richard Hawkins QC
Joseph Smiggers	Henry Dickens Hawksley CBE
Mr Blotton	Dr Robert Hawley CBE DSc FREng FRSE
Tom Roker	John Haynes
Nathaniel Winkle	Andrew Hearn ARICS
Mr Skimpin	John Heffernan BCom
Mr Simpson	Capt Christopher Hodgkinson FRAeS FRIN FRMetS
Bob Sawyer	John Holland CBE FCA JP DL (Deputy)
Mr Prosee	Peter Horrocks MA FRAS
Job Trotter	Jeremy Hyam BA (Hons)
Henry Beller	Graham Jackman
Mr Crawley	Edward Jackson
Jack Bamber	Sir Brian Jenkins GBE MA FCA FBCS
Mr Fogg	David Lancaster FCIS
Benjamin Allen	Alderman Sir David Lewis Kt MA

Frank Simmery	Paul Lloyd FSI
Tom Wildspark	The Rt Hon The Lord Mayor Alderman Ian Luder BSc (Econ) FCA FTII FRSA
Sam No. 924	Peter Lush FCA
Colonel Bulder	Sir Clive Martin Kt OBE TD DL
Joe the fat boy	Kenneth M McAllen
H Walker	John Mohin D.Univ FLJMU FRSA Dip.M FCIM
Mr Tom Martin	Malcolm Moss
Count Smorltork	John A Nash
Hunt	Ivan Nellist Dipl Arch RIBA FCIAug MInstM
Mr Luffey	Bruce Newbigging
Tommy	Alderman Sir Michael Oliver Kt LLD DLitt DL.
Pruffle	Peter M Olley C Eng FIStructE MICE
Muzzle	Colin J Parsons FCA
Thomas Burton	Antony Phillips FRICS
Dubbley	Geoffrey E Price (resigned)
Mr Clarke	Richard Pugh DL LLB FCA FCIS FRGS
Moses Pickwick	Gerald Pulman JP (Deputy)
Mr Raddle	Richard Regan ACIS CC (Deputy)
Scientific Gentleman	Professor David Rhind CBE FRS FBA DSc
The Hon Wilmot Snipe	David Shalit FCA
Mr Smithie	David Simmonds JP BSc FRICS
Mr Mivins	Sir Michael Snyder Kt FCA (Deputy)
Leo Hunter	Mark W Soundy BA
Mr Snicks	Alderman Sir John Stuttard Kt MA
Mr Namby	John Taylor TD
Crookey	Professor Michael Thorne BSc PhD FRSA
Captain Boldwig	Lawrence Turner OBE BSc CEng FIEE FCIBSE
Shiny Villiam	Richard Vardy FCIS ACIB MSI FRSA FRGS
Nathaniel Pipkin	Lord Wedgwood

Augustus Snodgrass
Harris
Jonas Mudge
Serjeant Buzfuz
Thomas Groffin
Mr Pott
Mr Pott
Alfred Jingle
Dr Slammer
Mr Wicks

Andrew Whitton
David Wickham MA FSA FRHistS
Brigadier Roy Wilde CBE
The late John Williams FCA
Philip Willoughby JP FCA (Deputy)
Michael Wilmot ACII
The late Tom Wilmot
Douglas Woodward CBE
Norman Woolley
Alderman David Wootton

Appendix 4
Immortal Memories

Speeches – to the Immortal Memory of Charles Dickens

11.3.63   Captain Peter G C Dickens DSO, DSC, RN

14.10.63   Lord Ilford

4.11.63   Mr Albert E Wilkins, President of the Southend and District branch of the Dickens Fellowship

10.2.64   Mr D W Ralph FRICS, AIStructE

9.3.64   Reverend C S Motley, Rector of St Michael's Cornhill

12.10.64   Mr William Latey MBE, QC

9.11.64   Rt Hon Lord Crook KStJ, JP

8.2.65   Mr Edgar Dennis Smith JP

8.3.65   Alderman Sir Gilbert Inglefield TD, MA

11.10.65   Mr John Greaves

8.11.65   Mr Ian M Leslie OBE, Editor of *The Builder*

14.2.66   Mr W E Rice CBE, JP

14.3.66   Mr Pickwick

10.10.66   Mr Dickson Wright MS, FRCS

7.11.66   Mr Eric Dickens Hawksley, President of the Dickens Fellowship

13.2.67   Mr Brian F Macdona

13.3.67   Harry Secombe

9.10.67   Very Reverend Martin G Sullivan, Dean of St Paul's

6.11.67   Mr William Latey QC

12.2.68   Mr J Rendel Jones MA (Oxon), Chief Education
Officer for East Sussex

11.3.68   His Honour Judge Gillis QC

14.10.68 Mr R J Minney

4.11.68   Chairman Capt Dowler read address from Mr D J W
Bridge

10.2.69   Mr Ashe Lincoln QC

10.3.69   Mr G A Peacock MA (Mr Remembrancer) (close
family ties with Charles Dickens through his wife)

13.10.69 Mr Tom Stoppard

3.11.69   Mr Harry Imrie Swainston (provided booklet to
every member of assembled company entitled *Proud
Heritage* which included thumbnail sketch of Charles
Dickens)

9.2.70   Mr Malcolm Andrews

9.3.70   Mr Pickwick

12.10.70 Mr Frank Allen

9.11.70   Sir Richard Thompson Bt, MP

8.2.71   Mr Christopher Serpell

8.3.71   Mr John Greaves, Hon Secretary of the Dickens
Fellowship

11.10.71 Reverend Canon Aidan Chapman TD, MA

Appendix 4 *Immortal Memories*

8.11.71   Mr Eric Dickens Hawksley

14.2.72   Mr William Addison JP, FSA

13.3.72   Alderman Kenneth Cork FCA

9.10.72   Mr John Brooke-Little MVO, MA, FSA

6.11.72   Mr D A Lyford

12.2.73   Mr Francis Crowdy

12.3.73   Mr Pickwick (Stanley Wells – his last meeting as Mr Pickwick)

8.10.73   Mr Julian Jeffs MA (Cantab), barrister-at-law

3.12.73   Dr Michael Fenton (Dr Payne)

11.2.74   Sir Desmond Heap

11.3.74   Reverend Basil A Watson OBE, MA, RN, Vicar of St Lawrence Jewry

14.10.74 Sir Carl Aarvold

2.12.74   Mr Roger Pincham

10.2.75   Mr Alvar Liddell

10.3.75   Mr David A Glen OBE, MA

13.10.75 Mr Stanley F Heather LLB, Comptroller and City solicitor

1.12.75   Mr Peter Drew, Chairman of the World Trade Organisation in London

9.2.76   Reverend A Mervyn Stockwood, Bishop of Southwark

8.3.76   Mr Norman L Hall CBE, LLB, Chairman of the Corporation Policy & Parliamentary Committee

11.10.76 Sir Norman Price CB, latterly Chairman of the Board of Inland Revenue

6.12.76   Mr Peter Davalle, Deputy Chief Foreign Sub-editor of *The Times*

7.2.77   Mr David Tucker MA

7.3.77   Mr A A Ross, Treasurer of Christ's Hospital

10.10.77   Sir William Pile KCB, MBE, Chairman of the Board of Inland Revenue

5.12.77   Master Jacob QC, the Queen's Remembrancer

13.2.78   Mr Alan S Watts, Hon Secretary of the Dickens Fellowship

6.3.78   Mr Ross Davies, Financial Editor of *The Times*

9.10.78   Mr Alistair Burnet (of ITV)

4.12.78   Mr Derrick G Cole

12.2.79   Mr John Melling

12.3.79   Sir David Floyd-Ewin MVO, OBE, MA, Deputy

8.10.79   Sir Richard Thompson Bt

3.12.79   Mr Geoffrey Johnson Smith MP

11.2.80   Mr Neil Thorne MP

10.3.80   Mr Stanley J Clayton, the Town Clerk

1.12.80   Rt Hon Lord Lloyd of Kilgerran

9.2.80   Mr Cedric Dickens, great-grandson of Charles Dickens (quaffing a glass of port purloined from his neighbour at table to illustrate a point)

9.3.81   Mr Stanley Heather CBE, lately Solicitor to the City Corporation

2.11.81   Professor Slome

7.12.81   Mr Peter Hemmings (many references to music in relation to Dickens' writings)

8.2.82   His Honour Judge Edward Clarke QC

8.3.82   Mr R J Attenborough CBE

6.12.82   Unrecorded

14.2.83   Unrecorded

14.3.83   Professor R L Williams MA, DPhil, DS, Director of the Metropolitan Police forensic science laboratory

10.10.83   Mr John Brooke-Little MVO, FSA, Norroy and Ulster King of Arms

5.12.83   His Honour Judge Michael Argylle

13.2.84   Mr Henry Collis MA

12.3.84   Mr Derek Baker MA, BLitt, FRHistS, Headmaster of Christ's Hospital

3.12.84   Mr Charles Mugleston (dressed as Charles Dickens and resembling him)

11.2.85   Mr John Rae, Headmaster of Westminster School

11.3.85   Mr Pickwick

14.10.85   Dr David Packer, Curator of Dickens House, 48 Doughty Street

2.12.85   Mr Christopher Bond

10.2.86   Mr E W J Tomlin CBE

10.3.86   Mr Nigel Stock (Mr Pickwick in the BBC production of *Pickwick Papers*)

17.11.86   Mr Kenneth McAllen

1.12.86   Mr John Cunningham, an international banker of repute

9.2.87   Mr Angus Watson

9.3.87   Mr Leslie Bowyer, Hon Treasurer of the Dickens
          Fellowship

12.10.87 Major Tony Young

7.12.87   Mr Robert Pearson

8.2.88   Mr Richard Dring, lately Editor of *Hansard* (with
          enlightening glimpses into Charles Dickens' own
          experiences as a parliamentary 'hack')

14.3.88   Dr David Hatch, consultant anaesthetist at Great
          Ormond Street hospital

5.12.88   Rear Admiral Richard Heaslip CB

13.2.89   His Excellency Rae Killen, South African ambassador

13.3.89   Mr Owen Kelly QPM, Commissioner of the City
          of London Police (a well-researched and often
          humorous discourse linking Dickens' writings with
          the development of policing practices in the City since
          Victorian times)

9.10.89   Sir Anthony Grant MP (a comparison of the lot of a
          Member of Parliament today with that in Dickens'
          day)

4.12.89   Mr Graham Storey (reminded his audience of the
          existence of a predecessor 'City Pickwick Club'
          founded in 1837 which used to meet at the Sun
          Tavern in Longacre. He went on to chronicle Dickens'
          endeavours, both as a speech-writer and reader of his
          own works in public)

12.2.90   Mr Richard York, Deputy Director of the Barbican
          Centre

12.3.90   Mr Alan S Watts, Hon General Secretary of the
          Dickens Fellowship

8.10.90   Right Honourable the Earl of Stockton (the audience
          was treated to a panoramic comparison of the social

scene today with that of Dickens' day. There was no doubt that had Dickens been alive in the 1990s he would still find many familiar topics for his brilliant observations including prison reform and education)

26.11.90 Mr Patrick Garland (a wide breadth of insights and comparisons of writing and performing in Dickens' time with those today)

4.2.91 Mr Melvyn Barnes, City Librarian

18.3.91 Mr Tim Owen, Principal Information Officer at the London Research Centre (a member of the Sherlock Holmes Society of London)

7.10.91 Mr Michael Cassidy (linked today's activity in various landmarks with their existence and importance in Dickens' day.

25.11.91 Mr Cedric Dickens (an illuminating and entertaining history of Dickens' early writings – *Sketches by Boz* (including the origin of that name) in 1836 and of course *Pickwick Papers* completed the following year)

3.2.92 Mr David Dickens (greatly stressed the Dickens family connection with the Navy – nine members of the family had served in the RN or RNVR – and based his dissertation around the topic of Charles Dickens as a champion of the underdog)

30.3.92 Right Reverend David Say KCVO, former Bishop of Rochester (gave ecclesiastical insights into the times in which Dickens was writing)

5.10.92 Mr Lionel Gracey FRCS (a panorama of the advances in medical science during Dickens' lifetime, including two of the greatest discoveries – anaesthesia and the control of infection especially during surgery)

23.11.92 Mr Peter Rees, City Planning Officer ('Dickens' London was still with us)

1.2.93 Mr Bryan Bass MA, Headmaster of the City of London School

29.3.93   Mr Eric Harrison, Master of the Charterhouse (gave a historical account of the Charterhouse which had been attacked by Dickens in his *Historical Words* in 1852)

4.10.93   Mr Cedric Dickens (a historical perspective of the life and times of Sir Henry Fielding Dickens and his wife (his grandparents). Sir Henry was Charles Dickens' son and was to become Common Serjeant of the City of London. Cedric Dickens had received the advice from him never to drink vintage port, always wood port)

29.11.93   Mr James Sewell, City Archivist

7.2.94   Dr Andrew Sanders, Reader in English at Birkbeck College

28.3.94   Very Reverend Eric Evans, Dean of St Paul's

10.10.94   Dr David Parker, Curator of the Dickens House Museum (told how the Bleeding Heart got its name and how the basis of the traditional menu was to be found in a cookery book written anonymously by Charles Dickens' wife)

28.11.94   Sir Lawrence Verney, Recorder of the City of London

6.2.95   Alderman Roger Cork

27.3.95   Mr Max Hebditch, Director of the City of London Museum (mention of the museum's location close to Newgate was made, whose historical significance was amply described by Charles Dickens in *Sketches by Boz*)

9.10.95   Mr Bernard Brooke-Partridge

27.11.95   Dr Jeremy Catto, Fellow of Oriel College, Oxford

5.2.96   Mr Roy Ullyett, doyen of sports cartoonists

25.3.96   Mr Tertius Metcalf

21.10.96   Mr Richard Ratner

Appendix 4 *Immortal Memories*

25.11.96 Mr A H P Gillett (a man much practised at impersonating Charles Dickens at readings at hospital Christmas parties)

10.2.97 Mr Desmond Fitzpatrick, Chairman of the City of London Historical Society

24.3.97 Captain Beauchamp ('Beacy') Blackett, Chairman of Ashdowns Fishmongers and Beauchamp's Restaurant in Leadenhall

13.10.97 Mr Donald Wilson, Stationmaster at Marylebone Station (reminded those present of Charles Dickens' escape from a major rail crash at Staplehurst in June 1866)

24.11.97 Mr Colin Parsons, Chairman of Taylor Woodrow

9.2.98 Mr Jerry Kirk, an eminent surgeon

30.3.98 Unrecorded

12.10.98 Deputy Rodney Fitzgerald

30.11.98 Unrecorded

1.2.99 Unrecorded

29.3.99 Unrecorded

27.9.99 Mr James Sewell MA, FSA, City Archivist

29.11.99 Mr David Bluett

31.1.00 The Venerable George Frost, Archdeacon of Lichfield (spoke on Little Nell and Tong, relating the tradition that the village of Tong was Little Nell's (from *The Old Curiosity Shop*) village)

27.3.00 Mr Cedric Dickens

12.6.00 (Ladies' Dinner) Mr Cedric Dickens

25.9.00 Mr Sheriff-elect Nigel Branson JP (spoke on Dickens, his novels and modern life)

27.11.00 Mr Philip Fisher, Administrator and General Secretary Birmingham and Midland Institute (spoke on the connections Dickens had with Birmingham and particularly with the Birmingham and Midland Institute)

29.01.01 His Honour Alan King Hamilton QC

26.3.01 Mr Bob Roberts (spoke on Dickens and the Iron Horse)

24.9.01 Mr Mike Petty, author, journalist, broadcaster (spoke about Mr Pickwick in Cambridge)

26.11.01 His Honour Judge Michael Hyam (spoke on the Chancery Court and other legal matters in Dickens' time)

28.1.02 Mr Dennis Turner, Chief Economist at HSBC Bank plc (spoke about the economy in the time of Dickens)

25.3.02 Mr Cedric Dickens

30.9.02 Mr Julian Jeffs QC (spoke on the descriptions of eating and drinking in *Pickwick Papers* and their effects on the characters)

25.11.02 Mr David Wickham MA, FSA, ARHistS (spoke on adaptations of Dickens' books)

27.1.03 His Honour Judge Peter Beaumont QC, the Common Serjeant (spoke on Charles Dickens and lawyers, and descriptions of them in *Pickwick Papers*)

24.3.03 Dr Rodney Edrich JP, BA, FRSA, FRGS (spoke on how his interest in Dickens arose and why he loved the books)

9.6.03 (Ladies' Dinner) Mr Cedric Dickens (gave some family reminiscences with detail about the *George and Vulture*)

22.9.03 Mr Henry Dickens Hawksley CBE (talked about what it was that made Charles Dickens great and why he had such an effect on the cultural life of the present day and how much he was revered even in his own lifetime)

24.11.03 Mr Deputy Michael Farrow MA, President of the City of London Historical Society (spoke about Dickens' influence on social reform, his amazing powers of description and his accounts of the perils of horse-drawn transport)

26.1.04 Dr Thomas Stuttaford OBE, Chief Medical Correspondent of *The Times*

22.3.04 Mr Desmond Shawe-Taylor, Director of the Dulwich Picture Gallery

14.6.04 (Ladies Dinner) Mr Derek L Davies CBE (spoke on Charles Dickens and the Athenaeum bringing in Thackeray, Ali Baba and the Forty Thieves and the clubs with which Dickens was associated)

27.9.04 His Honour Michael Mander DL

22.11.04 Mr Edward Walker-Arnott, Past Master of the Loriners Company

24.1.05 Major-General Sir Iain Mackay-Dick KCVO, MBE, Clerk to the Trustees and CEO of Morden College

21.3.05 Mr John Simpson, Chief Editor of the Oxford English Dictionary (who reviewed Dickens' pervasion of the dictionary)

26.9.05 Professor Malcolm Andrews, editor of *The Dickensian*

28.11.05 Lt-Cdr Mark G C Dickens RN, great-great-grandson of Charles Dickens, head of the Dickens family

23.1.06 Sir Alexander Graham GBE, Lord Mayor of London 1990–91, Chairman of the Trustees of Morden College

27.3.06 The Right Honourable the Lord Wedgwood

12.6.06 (In celebration of the life of Cedric Dickens) His Honour Judge Peter Beaumont QC, Recorder of London

25.9.06   Mr Timothy Ford, President of the University of Reading

27.11.06 His Honour Judge Richard Hawkins

22.1.07   Iain McWhirter BA (Hons) (spoke about the late President)

19.3.07   Dr Rodney Edrich JP, BA, FRSA, FRGS (gave an entertaining account of the cricket match between Old Muggleton and Dingley Dell)

24.9.07   Sir Robert Finch

26.11.07 Mr Jeremy Gotch MA (spoke about Mr Pickwick in Dulwich)

21.1.08   Mr William Shand MD, FRCS, FRCS (Edin) (spoke on Dickens' literary skills)

31.3.08   Mr John Heffernan